True Learning

A Renaissance To Establish
Authentic Learning

Trudi Carter

© 2023

When the heart
of the child
is touched by the love
of the teacher,
true learning takes place.

PREFACE

How is it possible to have so many different lessons and student stories plus a broad information background? Have the teacher change grade level assignments regularly, start with new curriculum or provide no curriculum, and allow the freedom to experiment. This creates many opportunities for original lessons and fresh student stories. As the teaching tactics are carried from one year to the next, they expand and enrich the methods of instruction. Over time, they consistently emphasize creating independent students who are successful thinkers.

With a broad array of school district teacher workshops based on new ideas, original concepts impact the classroom. Colleagues share methods they develop, university professors demonstrate the latest education techniques, and other school districts pass along their research results. An administrator who is asked, 'Why are the teachers given so many workshops?" answers, "The more arrows in the teacher's quiver, the more likely a new idea is implemented. The students benefit."

Creativity implements an idea and adjusts it as the situation warrants it. A willingness to add value to the students' learning in unique ways improves the teacher's instructional design. Schools build our future adults. With useful contributions to our communities, they provide leadership. They are foundational to a healthy and successful nation.

To provide consistency for the teacher in teaching the changing grade level assignments, an instructional model develops, *Teaching! It's all in the process*. Simplistic in design, quick and easy to implement in a variety of instructional situations, its basis is two-fold - student collaboration and comprehension through reasoning. With dozens of teaching options available, including the inspiration of the teacher, lessons become fresh, original, and yield successful learning techniques for the students.

To 'touch the heart of the child' gives each child the opportunity to learn well today and better tomorrow. An open-ended approach challenges the fast learner to go beyond the basics while the deliberate learner, who thoroughly processes each idea, is given time and examples to meet and exceed the criteria. This is 'with the love of the teacher.' 'True learning takes place' when students recognize their self-worth and succeed.

True Learning is a testimonial to a renaissance that leads to authentic learning. When every child knows their self-worth and how to contribute it to the world, there is a transformational impact on humanity.

With appreciation to all – especially the children,

Miss Trudi

CONTENTS

PART I
Teach Today

CHAPTER 1 *TEACHING! IT'S ALL IN THE PROCESS*
Base the teaching on student input
A Save the Sub B. The Teaching Process C. Analyze Answers
D. Presentation Options E. Student Collaboration
F. Summarize and Celebrate! G. An Answer Poem

CHAPTER 2 WE'RE ALL IN THIS TOGETHER
Collaborate with a team, a group, the class
A. Detectives Fix Mistakes B. Enrich Collaboration
C. Students Teach Science D. Students Edit E. A Play
F. 4 Boys Succeed G. Seize the Day
H. School Succuss

CHAPTER 3 MAKE IT EASY TO BE SMART
Achievement on grade level is true success
A. IQs Go Up B. Stay on Grade Level C. Surpass Sameness
D. Spelling Tactics E. Monotone Test F. Consider Shyness
G. Indoor Games H. 20 Questions I. Solve Mysteries

PART II
The Subjects

CHAPTER 4 REFLECT ON READING
Make inferences, then prove understanding
A. Dictate To Read B. Identify Implications C. Validate Facts
D. Memorize Poems E. Dr. Seuss F. Stages of Reading
G. Phases of Reading H. Reading Glitches

CHAPTER 5 CONSIDER WRITING
Train in the writing process, then begin
A. Floor Letters   B. Words From NZ   C. Frog Sentences
D. Copy to Write   E. Become an Author   F. First Time Writers
G. 5 Day Stories   H. Basic Report   I. Poetry   J. Haiku
K. Grade Papers Fast   L. Grading Rubric

CHAPTER 6 DISCOVER MATH
Start with hands-on, compute with reason
A 10 Facts   B. Long Addition   C. Multiplication Tactics
D. Finger Multiplication   E. Math Formulas   F. Coins   G. Time
H. Make Fractions   I. Compare Fractions
J. Measure Tree Height

CHAPTER 7 INVESTIGATE SCIENCE
Observe, identify a hypothesis, test
A. Compare Leaves   B. Count Leaves   C. Moth and Bugs
D. Bat, Snake, Fish   E. Light Bulbs   F. Measure Bubbles
G. Analyze Food Coloring   H. Observe Pendulums
I. Ants and Original Research   J. Arctic Bear

CHAPTER 8 FOUNDATIONS OF CIVILIZATION: SOCIAL
STUDIES & HISTORY
Begin with the individual, gain the greater good
A. Democracy   B. Petition   C. Majority Rule?   D. Analyze War
E. Mandan Research   F. Exchange Experts   G. Roman Empire
H. Market Place   I. Schoolhouse   J. Famous People
K. Conestoga Wagon

PART III
Enrichment Ideas

CHAPTER 9 CLASSROOM MANAGEMENT
Establish an organization for basics, then act
A. Clean Classroom   B. Hall Walking   C. ABCD's of Kindness
D. Assign Numbers   E. Study Teams   F. Spontaneity

CHAPTER 10 CLASSROOM SETTING AND ATMOSPHERE
Let the surroundings support the work
Part I.   A. Art B. Music C. Quotations   D. Fragrance
E. Room Designs … **Part II.**   F. Principal's Impact
G. Silent Signals   H. Gratitude and Praise   I. Fairness
J. Honesty   K. Trust   L. Mood

CHAPTER 11 A PLETHORA OF IDEAS
Perceive into and beyond the fundamentals
A. Plans   B. Decisions   C. Bloom 1,2,3   D. Bloom 4,5,6
E. Bloom's Chart   F. Thinking Techniques
G. 2-D Graphic Designs   H. AVK Learning   I. 7 Intelligences

CHAPTER 12 #REALSTORIESHAPPEN
Respond with authority; continue with caring
A. No Diploma   B. Change in Behavior
C. Compassion for Richard D. Alexa   E. Handle Sickness
F. Amazing Question G. Lesson Washout
H. A Career Concludes

Index
Sources
Miss Trudi's Bio
A Student's Perspective

BENEFITS of TRUE LEARNING

To affect the next generation of adults, a true education must begin now For the homeschool parent, *True Learning* ensures the child is receiving the benefits of a full and proper education. In the classroom, *True Learning* infuses the curriculum with authentic learning techniques.

Examining this book's quotations and sharing the supporting stories, adults lead children to become fully functioning learners. With the detailed information and thinking techniques, children are prepared to be effective adults able to access and apply their life choices. Based on *True Learning,* the students will –

* Develop interpersonal skills with peers.
  * Expand the learning process with a study partner.
  * Recognize self-worth and its value to independent learning.
  * Contribute to group activities.
  * Present explanations to the class.
  * Appreciate varying viewpoints.
* Gain understanding and success with proper scholastic tools.
  * Apply advanced levels of questioning.
  * Identify long range implications.
  * Apply techniques to communicate clearly and effectively.
  * Utilize a variety of memory retention methods.
  * Validate facts through research.

As a teacher provides multiple opportunities for a child's success.
The heart of the child is touched by the love of the teacher,
and true learning takes place.

PART I
Teach Today

The First Day

Chapter 1 *Teaching! It's all in the process*

Chapter 2 *We're all in this together*

Chapter 3 *Make it easy to be smart*

THE FIRST DAY

The first day of my teaching career begins without a plan or a clue as to what to do when the students enter the room. Arriving in the classroom at 9:00 a.m. - the required time - the 9:15 school bell soon rings. Twenty-one 4th graders file quietly into the room. Each child sits down at a desk and folds their hands. Their self-disciplined behavior reflects their parents' expectations. The sea of faces looks expectantly at their new teacher.

After writing my name on the board, I turn back to face the children and say, "Good morning. I'm Miss Carter." At that point, there is no plan as to what to say or do next. Deciding to be honest, my dilemma is explained. "I worked overseas this summer. My return flight was delayed until yesterday afternoon. As you can see there's nothing on the bulletin boards and no agenda on the chalkboard. Will you help me?"

The words 'Will you help me?' become the fundamental theme for the rest of my career. If the curriculum is unfamiliar or seems too difficult for the children, the students are asked to provide assistance. Students love to help, to be involved in the lesson, to prove themselves important and capable.

A 4th grader offers to help. Following her directions, the class list is numbered – 101, 102, etc. Each set of books is also numbered and another child delivers the books. Spelling books, math workbooks, and textbooks now have a tracking method similar to bar codes and magnetized strips. After taking them home to check, they will be easy to return to the proper child. Next, the children switch their seats until they are seated alphabetically starting from right front to back left.

As the year goes on, student participation in their lessons increases. They help each other with assignments and explain the meanings of information on the chalkboard. An opportunity for further independent work happens when a box containing SRA (Science Research Associates) Reading Laboratory cards is found. Tested and assigned to a reading level, each child reads an information or story card daily and answers questions about the details and grammar. I check their answers and record their scores. The more students take part in their lessons, the higher are their test grades.

Authentic learning is based on how to think and teach each other. The teacher's role is to give the children the scholastic skills to learn and provide opportunities to be independent learners.

Miss Trudi

Chapter 1
Teaching! It's all in the process

Base the teaching on student input

Topics
A Save the Sub   B. The Teaching Process   C. Analyze Answers
D. Presentation Options   E. Student Collaboration
F. Summarize and Celebrate!   G. An Answer Poem

Introduction

To teach students the techniques to learn independently and the skills to teach each other creates a roomful of assistant teachers. The teacher provides curriculum, and the students collaborate based on thinking strategies.

Serendipity steps in. A music substitute rushes into the library, she asks for help in expanding a 15 minute lesson. Suddenly, the 'student-focused teaching techniques' solidify into a logical instructional design. Step by step how to involve the students is explained. Though her class lessons range from 2nd to 5th grade, she proves the effectiveness of the new instructional design.

Teaching! It's all in the process becomes the foundation for my career. From academically gifted students to a tutoring business, this process brings out the talents and higher level thinking skills of every learner. Success for the child is independent learning and self-worth. Success for the teacher is a clear, succinct teaching procedure.

I have come to believe that a teacher is a great artist.
Teaching might even be the greatest of the arts since the medium
is the human mind and spirit.
John Steinbeck

1001.A SAVE THE MUSIC SUBSTITUTE

An Instructional Design

A substitute rushes up just before school starts. "I need help!" she says in a slightly panicked voice. "I'm the music substitute. All I have is this 15 minute video about Bach. The classes are 45 minutes long and range from 2nd to 5th grade. Please help me." A teaching process based on student participation is shared.

Step 1. Establish expectations

After the students sit down, tell them to put their name on a piece of paper and the number of their class session. Say, "At the end of this class, you'll be asked to write the answer to one question and turn it in. You will all know the answer."

Step 2. Introduce the topic

"In the middle of the board, write the word 'Bach' and ask, "What are the details of a person's life?" Around the name, write their ideas such as birth place, birth date, successes, challenges, and date of death. Compliment their contributions.

Say, "As you watch the Bach video, pay attention to the details, and write a few notes on the back of your paper. At the end of the video, we'll put your details next to the ideas on the board."

Step 3. Show the video.

Step 4. Debrief the video.

After the video, reread their *original topics* on the board, then say, "Share with your neighbor something you learned about Bach." After a short time ask, "What details do you recall?" As the students contribute their answers, write the key words next to the original topics. Compliment their responses.

Step 5. Summarize and celebrate.

Tell the students, "On the front of your paper, write one sentence to explain why we should remember Bach today. Use an idea from the board or one of your own." Then say, "Tell what you wrote about Bach why." To encourage sharing, nod and smile.

Step 6. Finally say, "Let's celebrate your good work with silent applause." Demonstrate a 'silent circle clap.' Have the children join in.

Step 7. "As the class leaves, stand by the door to collect their papers. Use the names on the papers to speak directly to them such as, 'Thanks, Raymone. I'm glad you were here today! Sylvia, your idea was great." Smile a lot! At recess and lunch, the next classes will hear how terrific you are and look forward to your class.

At the end of the day, the sub returned with a big smile on her face. "Even with the different grade levels, every class went well. Thank you." Before going home, she reviewed the papers and drew a red star on each one. No failures. With answers recorded on the board, a 'successful sentence' was guaranteed.

Summary
When students do the teaching and learning, everyone succeeds at their ability level. Clear expectations, interesting information, student collaboration, and a teacher's summary result in a successful lesson. Praise to honor their efforts and a celebration inspires self-worth.

Teaching! It's all in the process! is key to long term learning and lifelong skills. As students take a larger role in their learning, grades improve. Why? Because teaching information to others requires a high level of understanding. Those who teach get smarter, let the children teach.

The one exclusive sign of thorough knowledge
is the power of teaching.
Aristotle

Reference Codes
As information is rearranged during the writing of this book, it impacts the page numbers and the index. Therefore, reference codes are used to identify a lesson. For instance,

1005.C FROG SENTENCES. 2 TO 22 WORDS.
    5 is the 5th chapter
    C is the alphabetical order (3rd lesson)
    FROG SENTENCES. 2 TO 22 WORDS is the title.

Dialogue
A sample of teacher and student dialogue clarifies a lesson.

Quotations
The quotes in this book follow copyright rules which require that they are spoken by someone who lived more than 50 years ago.

1001.B *TEACHING! IT'S ALL IN THE PROCESS*

4 Key Steps
1* Question 2* The Presentation 3* Collaboration 4* Summarize and Celebrate!

TEACHING! IT'S ALL IN THE PROCESS ...A BRIEF OVERVIEW

1* The Open-Ended Question
A broad question with lots of answers engages all students. Try out the question ahead of time to be sure there are many answers.
1007.J THE ARCTIC OR THE POLAR BEAR?

2* The Presentation
Either the teacher or the students present the information. In this lesson, the students teach the textbook.
1002.C STUDENTS AS SCIENCE TEACHERS

3* Collaboration
Focused team discussions develop in-depth thinking and creativity which improve understanding. In this lesson, groups learn and apply the value of coins.
1006.F COINS AND ALGEBRA

4* Summarize and Celebrate!
A review of key ideas includes details and implications. Celebrate the students' success with praise. A list of praise words are in 1010.H. Use them, too, for compliments when grading papers. A celebration ranges from precise compliments to a reward.

Learning is not attained by chance; it must be sought for with ardor and diligence.
Abigail Adams

Summary
This 4-step instructional design is the foundation for interactive and collaborative teaching. Students, totally involved, have no time to claim boredom. Lessons 1001.C to 1001.F expand and enrich these 4 steps.

Action is the foundational key to all success.
Pablo Picasso

TEACHING! IT'S ALL IN THE PROCESS ... THE DETAILS

1001.C THE OPEN-ENDED QUESTION - INCREASE ANSWERS
The Teaching Process. Step 1

Students' wave their hands a lot when the teacher's question has lots of answers.

- What words refer to weather?
- What do pioneers need to know for the 3 month trip West?
- Which animals live in the ocean?
- How many ways can we write a number sentence that equals 5?

Guidelines
- Set time limits. Creative thinking easily fills an entire class period.
- Include domino, variety, and distinct to make a class lesson longer
- Record answers in plain sight. Participation goes up when students see their answers written for everyone else to see.

These 3 activities increase the students' *purposeful thinking* to find more answers, 'domino,' 'variety,' 'distinct.'

*Domino
As dominos fall one onto the other, so one answer triggers another.

TEACHER "Jaylynn is using a new thinking technique. When the word 'bee' is written on the board, she says, 'pollen.' The word bee suggests pollen as bees carry pollen from flower to flower. This type of thinking is called 'domino' because one answer suggests another. Let's look over our answers and add 'domino' words."

*Variety
To prove there are a 'variety' of answers, connect similar answers with lines, then count the groups. The more groups, the larger the variety.

TEACHER "Let's sort our words for outer space by creating mini-groups of similar words. I'll draw the connecting lines. Then, let's think of a similar word for each group."

STUDENTS " star-comet…(sun)   planet-asteroid…(moon) constellation-solar system…(galaxy)."

TEACHER "When you mentally connect similar words, it helps you think of a new word. This technique is called 'variety.'"

*Distinct
Sometimes there is an answer that fits the question, but there is no similar word. This stand-alone word is called a 'distinct' answer.

TEACHER "We connected similar weather words such as mist, humidity, and rain. Which word on the board isn't connected?"
STUDENT "Thunder."
TEACHER "Yes. Because there is no similar word for 'thunder,' it's called 'distinct.' Distinct answers match the question, but stand alone."

Note. Students contribute a 'far out' answer when they realize it may be 'distinct.'

To Eliminate Words
An answer is removed gracefully as the class analyzes their answers. Catching on to this activity, students are more likely to contribute an answer even though it may be erased later.

TEACHER "Wow! Look at all these words about outer space. Let's identify the best words for your outer space report. I'll put a check mark by the words you want, and erase the words you say don't fit. A question mark means we can't decide."

Summary
The open-ended question is a true marvel. It involves all students, improves their ability to listen and think, and provides a solid base of words or ideas for an activity. Apply the 3 'answer patterns' and analytical thinking improves. With this type of question, children wave their hands to give answers, and find it fun to be smart.

An open-ended question at the beginning of a new unit or lesson gathers ideas and finds out what students *already know*. This saves teaching time. Ask the question in the middle of a lesson, and students review the material and are prepared for the next information. Finally, use the question as a review at the end of a lesson or unit.

Question everything. Learn something. Answer nothing.
Euripides

Author. Answer nothing? Laughter.

1001.D PRESENTATION OPTIONS
The Teaching Process Step. 2

A presentation tells the information to be learned. These 9 techniques provide variety; the students take notice; and the day flies by.

*1 Capture Curiosity
Challenge students' imagination with unusual information.
- A unique fact about microscopic animals. *Did you know…?*
- Artwork from the time period. *What does this painting tell us about the Revolutionary War?*
- A little known fact about a person or event. *This unique fact about… explains….*
- Regalia such as a cowboy hat, a Victorian hourglass, or a map. *Check this item out. It shows us that….*

- For a nature lesson, show Audubon's artwork found online. *How does this bird fit into its environment?*
- For the ocean, layer transparencies to create the shoreline and show marine life. *What type of animals live along the shore? How do their characteristics help them survive?*

*2 Lecture with AVK
Education research defines 3 ways to learn: hearing (auditory), seeing (sight), or through an activity (kinesthetic). A presentation reflects the children's learning preferences. *Auditory learners* 'tell and discuss' information. *Visual learners* look at a list of key ideas or a map. *Kinesthetic learners* 'act out' key information or 'watch others in action.'
1011.H HOW LEARNING HAPPENS - AVK

Story
The middle school students in the enrichment program encourage a visit their favorite teacher. Watching his lesson, it's clear the students are listening intently. His teaching technique is unique. As he lectures, he tells *'out loud'* what he is thinking. Talking *about* his understanding, the children learn the 'process of what is happening in his head.' The students are intrigued, fully engaged - and learning how to think.

*3 Teams of Two
Pairs of students are assigned to read paragraphs from the textbook, then share the information.
1002.C STUDENTS AS SCIENCE TEACHERS

*4 Video
1001.A SAVE THE MUSIC SUBSTITUTE

*5 Secondary Research
The teacher reads selections and the sources from a variety of books related to the curriculum. This expands background information and teaches the process for secondary research.

*6 Related Images
Photographs of people referred to in the lesson as well pictures of the environment where the situation takes place provide mental pictures that make the lesson more realistic.
1005.I PHOTOS TO POETRY

*7 Graphics
Graphics interpret information in a new way. For instance, to explain how the flower makes a seed, students draw and label the parts of a flower including how that part works.
1011.G 2-D GRAPHIC DESIGNS

*8 Beyond Knowledge
Interest pops when new information goes beyond basic facts, opinions, and data. The *extra explanation* locks curriculum information into the learner's long term memory.
1008.F BECOME AN EXPERT

*9 Storytelling
Stories shift student memory into high gear. As storytelling includes dialogue, visual descriptions, and action events, the AVK learners find that recall is effortless.
1008.J FAMOUS PEOPLE AND FASCINATING FACTS

Summary
With 9 presentations and original additions, *Teaching! It's all in the process* provides originality and freshness. From lectures to videos to regalia, teaching becomes the 'art of combinations.'

Story
One winter, my brother constantly studied a book about his new hobby.

While the winter winds blow, he sailed his boat around Merrick Bay in his imagination.

With the arrival of warm temperatures and sunny days, he jumped into his boat and sailed off toward the horizon. Imagining himself in the boat zooming across the water handling wind and waves in the Winter, made it easy to sail for the first time in the Spring.

Note. A thorough verbal description of an activity prepares students for the activity to come. Hmm. 'Mentally picturing an activity' must be the 10th option for teaching a lesson.

> *Adopt the pace of Nature, her secret is patience.*
> Ralph Waldo Emerson

1001.E STUDENT COLLABORATION
The Teaching Process Step. 3

Collaboration goes beyond conversation to identify new connections that develop understanding. Merriam-Webster's online definition of collaboration is, 'the act of working together, a united labor - especially in literary or scientific work.'

> *"Coming together is a beginning, keeping together is progress; working together is success."*
> Edward Everett Hale

Talking together can easily morph into "What's for lunch?" Guided by the process of collaboration, students share ideas, listen, ask questions, and appreciate differing viewpoints. The ability to communicate ideas with everyone, everywhere, leads to better relationships in family and school.

Listening Techniques

Communication includes an ability to recognize and use listening signals. These silent and verbal signals prove 'someone is listening.'

*Visual Signals
- Head nods up and down.
- Kind smiles.
- Puzzled look, a question asked.
- A thumbs up!
- A silent clap.

*Verbal Signals
- That's a good idea.
- Yes, and let's think about….
- Please tell me more…
- I like that.

Collaboration Guidelines
- Timing. Such as a 2 minute limit.
- Specific directions. "After brainstorming, write down your words."
- Take turns.
- Practice listening signals - verbal and visual.
- Ask questions to be sure your understanding is clear.

In these 3 collaborative lessons, the children have a wonderful time working and learning together. It's the joy factor of learning so to speak.
1003.H 20 QUESTIONS. TERRIFIC THINKERS!
1005.F THIRD GRADERS. FIRST TIME WRITERS.
1006.F COINS AND ALGEBRA

Story
Stepping into a classroom of 7th graders drawing and debating a math problem is an amazing experience. The math problem is, "How many cuts are needed to saw a log into four equal pieces?" Desks are pushed together into groups of 4. Mr. Williams sits up front listening and calling out suggestions. Asking for volunteers, a group comes forward, papers in hand, to explain how they solved the problem.

Taking turns, the group explains their answer and how it is proved. They even show what doesn't work! To put it mildly, they are impressive. Had these students been in a meeting with CEOs, they would have held their own. The class then asks questions. The teacher asks questions. This is far beyond a simple math presentation.

Later, Mr. Williams explains that he transformed his entire math curriculum into collaborative activities. Full participation in his classes is a given. The best part? According to him, learning to think effectively and creatively improves their national ITBS test scores. Collaboration and analysis leads to figuring out answers on tests.

Summary
For children, collaboration and conversation are similar. However, conversations wander about in and out of cul-de sacs with no special goal. To emphasize collaboration, set a goal such as, "Write 2 sentences about the relationship between bees and pollen."

Why use collaboration?
- Thinking strategies improve. *Better, faster learners!*
- Learning is rock-solid. *Recall is terrific! Test scores improve!*
- Lessons are more interesting. *Students are involved. Hooray!*

...the day is coming when telegraph wires will be laid into houses...and friends will discourse with each other without leaving home.
Alexander Graham Bell

1001.F SUMMARIZE AND CELEBRATE!
The Teaching Process. Step 4

*Summaries
These range from 'teacher guided' to student teamwork. Or connect

information into a unique whole such as a webbing. (see Chapter 11 for 2-D Graphic Designs) A summary happens naturally when students apply the information's details to a creative activity such as a time line, As the results are shared, students celebrate their success. Young children may want to applaud.

*Celebrate!
For the child, completing an assignment properly is success. Even a 'moment of recognition' reminds children they are capable and did well. A silent clap or a self-pat on the back builds confidence. Lunch in the classroom honors their work. Students love a celebration to acknowledge their effort.

Options
- The office or lunchroom staff is invited to see the students present their work.
- Students parade their work through a class of younger children, who will look forward to doing the activity in the upper grade.
- Videotape their results. As children may worry about being filmed, this is used as an option. It is shown during a rainy day recess.
- Special food treats, extra time at recess, or eating lunch in the classroom with friends are all welcome ways to celebrate a job well done.
- Or just shout 'Hooray!' and move on.
1010.H GRATITUDE AND PRAISE

*He who would learn to fly one day must first learn
to stand and walk and run and climb and dance,
one cannot fly into flying.*
Friedrich Nietzsche

1001.G AN ANSWER POEM
Children want to give the right answer. This didactic poem guarantees success.

A Success-Filled Moment

The teacher's spoken question flies about the room.
The children sit so still.

A pause to think.
To watch for the nod that comes and
leaning toward a friend,
in twos silently they speak.

A number taken from the jar, is called out.
A child's eyes sparkle.
"Check your answer with someone,"
gives permission
to visit another student's desk.

Busy whispers and nodding heads confirm the answer.
Returning to the desk, the student stands tall,

"The answer is…"
and it is right!

It is not so much our friends' help that helps us,
as the confidence of their help.
Epicurus

Summary
Encourage students to confirm an answer any time - except during a test!
:) Assured in knowing the answer leads to confidence in completing the
assignment.

CHAPTER 1 IN CONCLUSION
TEACHING! IT'S ALL IN THE PROCESS

In the one room school house, the teacher is a mentor, guide, and the source of knowledge. Students explain answers to each other, figure out assignments together, and celebrate their accomplishments. This teaching process produces capable citizens.
1008.A THE ONE ROOM SCHOOLHOUSE

Today, students must learn to participate fearlessly. Sharing research-based information with others, they develop self-assurance. Working in teams, they radiate confidence. Soon, they are independent learners. These future citizens are the backbone of a successful nation.

Give a man a fish and you feed him for a day.
Teach a man to fish, and you feed him for a lifetime.
Maimonides

Chapter 2

We're all in this together

Collaborate with a team, a group, the class

Topics
A. Detectives Fix Mistakes   B. Enrich Collaboration
C. Students Teach Science   D. Students Edit   E. A Play
F. 4 Boys Succeed   G. Seize the Day   H. School Success

Introduction
As students research facts, prepare lessons, and teach their each other, they develop reasoning skills and ingenuity. Positive group experiences lead to competent children.

Collaboration - taught, understood, and demonstrated - leads to fine-tuned roles in leadership and followship. A student's future is bright when an interviewer asks, "Do you work well with others?" and descriptions of team and group success is described.

It is true. *How to do* a job can be trained starting on the first day of employment. *How to work well with others* is a character trait that develops at home and school. The education system must contribute to developing effective employees and future citizens.

> *If everyone is moving forward together,*
> *then success takes care of itself.*
> Henry Ford

1002.A STUDENT DETECTIVES FIX MISTAKES
A fix-it detective is a student taught to identify and correct grammar and math mistakes including those on a test. First, the teacher trains the students to correct math and grammar mistakes. Next, the students earn

extra credit for correcting their test mistakes after it is returned.

Collaboration with their classmates in learning math and writing rules makes it easier for students to gain long term memory. Eventually, the students correct each other's work. Over time, alert to correcting mistakes, the youngsters make fewer mistakes.

*Grammar fix-its
The 'fix-it' grammar assignment begins when the students enter the room in the morning. On the overhead/smartboard are 3 sentences with grammar and spelling mistakes. At the end of each sentence is a number in parentheses that indicates how many mistakes are to be found and corrected. Identifying the mistakes, the students rewrite the sentences properly and underline the corrected mistakes. Becoming better 'detectives,' the students soon spot and correct their own mistakes as they write.

Note. By using social studies or science sentences, new facts are introduced or reviewed. Double learning happens.

Example
Mistakes
   The flock of fish swiming along the eqator enjoyed the warme atlantic current. (5)
Corrections
   The <u>school</u> of fish <u>swimming</u> along the <u>equator</u> enjoyed the <u>warm</u> <u>Atlantic</u> current.

Results
Confidence abounds as students explain the grammar corrections to the class. Drawing a red star above their own correction indicates a successful 'fix.' Scores are recorded at the top. (15 mistakes? 12 corrected? +12/15) Although the scores aren't counted as grades, they

indicate to the teacher which writing rules need to be reviewed. What a multipurpose assignment this is!

*Math Fix-its
Based on the math unit, students are given 3 math problems with mistakes. The detectives analyze the steps and make corrections. As the students explain their corrections, it becomes an introduction or a review for the math lesson.

Benefits of 'fixing'
  - Expectations are consistent and fair.
  - 'Fixing' provides an intense focus on specific rules.
  - Hanging around the hallways decreases. Students need every minute for the fix-it time.
  - Able to spot teacher-generated mistakes, students spot their own and, later on, each other's.
  - 100% participation. Everyone is paying attention.
  - Able to identify, correct, and explain mistakes, students better understand how the rules work.
  - Repetition, practice, and analysis results in long term recall.

Correcting their test mistakes
The students enjoy earning extra points on their test after it is returned. But how do they know the correct answers?

Step 1. After collecting the finished tests, a copy is placed on the overhead. Reviewing the test, students explain the answers in teams or as a class. Knowing they can earn extra points later, there is 100% attention.

Asking questions, especially if they disagree, locks the correct answer into memory.

Step 2. When checking the tests, the teacher checks the wrong answers without an explanation of the right answer.

Step 3. After the tests are returned, the students correct their mistakes. The correction time is based on the length of the test.

Step 4. BONUS. If a student writes a brief explanation as to why the answer is wrong and is now right, another point is given.

Examples
- I spelled 'Europe' wrong, I forgot the 'u'
- The noun and verb didn't match, I forgot the 's.'
- In adding, I forgot to carry the 2 in the 2nd column.
- The times fact was 9x5 = 45, not 44.

Knowing and explaining the correct answers pays off on future tests and school assignments.

What if the test is already perfect?
The A students are challenged to write a unique question, its answer, and a brief explanation of the right answer. The new test score reflects the bonus points such as A^{+5} For a good student, it's amazing to have a test go beyond an A.

Note. Although points for corrections are given, a test grade can only go up *one grade*. Record keeping indicates the correction points. C^{+6} ...B

Story
T review for a test, the substitute handed out the test! She literally told the students the answers. Returning the next day, I was dismayed. Would

everyone get an A? However, being told the answers is not the same as learning them. There was no positive impact on the test scores.

Summary
No one wants to be 'a failure forever.' To get an answer right the 2nd time around, and know why it's right, leads to more effort to get it right the first time. As the students review the test answers, they better understand how a question and answer works together.

Future employers will be grateful for an employee who learns from their mistakes, then corrects them. CEOs are made of this.

Note. When a test is handed out, consider saying, "You are all doing better at correcting. Take your time on the test." This prevents the student from thinking, "Oh, it's okay if I get it wrong, I can get it right later."

Mistakes are the portals of discovery.
James Joyce

1002.B BUTTERFLIES EXCEL AT COLLABORATION

Super-involved study teams are totally into learning. Collaboration develops reasoning skills and superior levels of understanding. From 'fact knowledge' to 'evaluation of ideas,' clarity and depth are the keys.

A pupil's progress is proven by higher scores on national tests such as the ITBS. This ability to reason, applied to school work and demonstrated through activities, lasts for a very long time.
1001.E COLLABORATION
1011.C AND D BLOOM 1,2,3 AND 4,5,6

Research on collaboration
At NYC University, Cecelia Reddington and Raymond Canada set-up an action research to *'compare the level of math success to the level of*

student participation'. Positive test results proved that participation is key to math achievement.

Results in hand, the researchers encourage teachers to develop a child-centered environment in which students perform math investigations together.
1001.E COLLABORATION - MR. WILLIAMS' MATH GROUPS

More collaboration research
In his book, *The Secret of Our Success:…"* Joseph Henrich notes that a smart species needs a "cultural infrastructure to share, to teach, to learn." In other words, collaboration.

Henrich points out that students must be taught *how to* interact with others in order to improve understanding. His 'investigative research' includes effective question techniques. (see Chapter 11 C and D)

Now. Let us stop for a moment and, with *substitutions and the condensing of his ideas*, read a brief summary of Henrich's explanation of the 'social importance and impact' of working collaboratively with others.

Consider two populations, the Geniuses and the Butterflies. Mathematically, the Geniuses invent a device or an amazing contribution to society once in 10 lifetimes. 1:10 The Butterflies are less smart and only invent or contribute a wonderful idea once in 1000 lifetimes. 1:1000

Comparing the ratios, the Geniuses are 100 times smarter than the Butterflies. 10 (Butterflies) x *100* = 1000 (Geniuses) But the Geniuses are quite shy and have only one friend they can learn from. 1:1 However, the Butterflies are more social (collaborative) and have 10 friends which makes them 10 times more social. 1:10

Now, everyone in both the Genius and the Butterfly population wants to succeed either by doing the work independently or by working with a friend. The important question is, *Which population will devise the most inventions and contributions to society?* Does collaboration make a difference?

Results
For the Geniuses a bit fewer than 1 out of 5 individuals (18%) will succeed in creating an invention. However, only half of that group, or 9%, succeed by themselves. 9:100

Meanwhile, 99.9% of the Butterflies succeed in developing an invention or amazing contribution to society. However, only 0.1% figured it out completely by themselves. .01:100

Questions
How does real success happen? With over 99% of the Butterflies contributing to a successful invention, it is clear - *collaboration counts.*

Wouldn't it be grand to work with another person - collaborate - and succeed 99.9 % of the time? 99.9:100

Note. Collaboration guidelines are in Chapter 1, 1001.E
Note. Taught to enrich collaboration with study and the investigative skills found in Chapter 11, students develop a high level of confidence. Team accomplishment supports future 'independent success.'
1011.G 2-D GRAPHIC DESIGNS

Summary
Collaboration develops 'people skills' which include sharing ideas, asking questions, and explaining one's viewpoint. Specific techniques based on nonverbal skills enrich team work. These skills improve family interactions, work experiences, and a people-centered activities.

This author's definition of collaboration.
"A shared free flowing of ideas on a topic headed for an agreed upon goal while wandering in and out of rabbit holes with Alice and stopping off in cul-de-sacs where unique ideas abound."

Conversation – a definition
"An exchange of thoughts in which understanding is gained when both participants achieve identical perspectives. *Sameness is the goal.*"
Source. Noah Webster's 1828 Dictionary

Note. Mr. Webster spent his entire life in the 1800's investigating and recording the English language in America. His definitions are thorough for his time. His large dictionary is almost 4 inches thick.

Collaboration and conversation - each has its purpose and unique results. Why not choose to be a Butterfly and converse and collaborate with everyone?

> *Conversation about the weather is the last refuge*
> *of the unimaginative.*
> Oscar Wilde

1002.C Students As Science Teachers

A high school teacher asks for a lesson to observe *Teaching! It's all in the process* in his science class. The underlying question is, "Will high school students learn information in teams, and then teach their classmates?"

The lesson
The class comes in, sits down, and stares blankly. One fellow puts his head down on his arms and appears to fall asleep. The science teacher hands me the textbook and assignment. Glancing at it, I see the topic is ecosystems.

Introducing myself and asking questions about what they learned yesterday, an open-ended question is written on the board, "What are the components and interactions of ecosystems?" A few brief responses are recorded. It's time to give the learning and teaching to the students.

First, the students are asked to find a partner. The napping student joins a nearby classmate. Next, each pair is assigned a paragraph from the textbook. The directions are, "For the next 15 minutes, read and record the main ideas. Create one test question, its answer and its explanation. Your information will be shared with the class." The quiet talking is encouraging.

After 15 minutes, their presentations begin. Students stand, tell their information, and ask their question. If someone knows the answer, they give it. If not, the answer is given and explained. After they take their turn, a brief compliment is given. "That idea is clear." "Your question is on target." When the bell rings, I thank them for being a great class to teach. They leave the room smiling.

Summary
The science teacher is enthusiastic. He comments, "I hadn't realized a lesson can be taught by the class. As they gave the presentations, I saw a new role for myself - coordinator."
1001A Save the Substitute

With collaboration, comes freedom from fear. If an answer is unknown, it's figured out in a team. Plus, understanding is individualized by each child - no sameness here.
1001.G An Answer Poem

The art of teaching is the art of assisting discovery.
Mark Van Doren

1002.D STUDENTS AS EDITORS

The 5th graders' assignments are written poorly. Specific grammar lessons have no effect as the students have no desire to write properly. I wonder, "Would writing improve if the students became editors?" Logically speaking, learning the skills to edit each other's papers, students should improve in writing their own papers.

To introduce the editing process, 3 types of writing samples are composed. The students will analyze each one.

*Sample 1: What is done well?
A well-written story is placed on the overhead. After the study teams read it, the question is posed, "What parts of this story are done well?" The teams collaborate. As the class shares their compliments, they are recorded on a chart - with flair!

"I like the title," is beefed up to 'Fascinating title!' 'This idea is new" translates to 'Superb new idea.' "The ending is a surprise" becomes 'Fantastic surprise ending!'

Fascinating title! Superb new idea! Fantastic surprise ending! Amazing details! Logical flow of ideas! Unique vocabulary! Excellent action words! Appropriate! Incredible sentences! Superb spelling! Unique twists! Well arranged!

As their basic remarks turn into exciting compliments, the class is laughing - and paying close attention.

*Sample 2: What needs improvement?
The poorly written essay is put up. Due to its many spelling and grammar mistakes, it's read aloud. The question is asked, "What needs to be improved?" The teams collaborate.

Laughter erupts as they find silly mistakes. As the class shares their results, their contributions are recorded on a 2nd chart. It's clear they recognize grammar and spelling mistakes. Their critiques include,

> Title doesn't fit. Ending fades away. Detail is incomplete. Better details needed. Out of order. Fact doesn't belong. Poor spelling. Wrong words that sound alike. Odd comment. Poor grammar. Boring vocabulary.

> *The most wasted of all days is the one without laughter.*
> e. e. cummings

Note. The 5th grade grammar book is a source for making typical and ridiculous mistakes. Textbooks are available online.

*Sample 3: 3 compliments, 2 critiques
One more essay is presented. This time the requirements are specific: identify 3 compliments and 2 suggestions for improvement. Two support questions are written on the board to clarify the editing process, "What's terrific?" "What needs to be improved?"

The study teams edit the essay. When the class shares their results, the edits are stopped at 3 terrific ideas, and 2 suggestions for improvement.

*Sample 4: A student's writing
For this lesson, a student volunteers his/her writing. Because the number of critiques allowed is limited, the study teams are reminded to identify 'key' compliments or improvements.

Independence
Understanding this process, study teams edit each other's papers. The editors sign their names at the bottom over the title "Senior Editor." Twice a week, student writing is contributed for class editing.
1011.G 2-D GRAPHIC DESIGNS - CHARTS

Story

Elizabeth, a 5th grader, is a poor writer. During the editing lessons based on students' writing, she observes the process intently. One day during an editing session, her hand flies up. "Editing helps. I want my paper to be put up for the class to edit." The class is kind in explaining their compliments and improvements. Elizabeth's writing skills begin to flourish.

Note. Kindness is emphasized as a part of editing. Compliments and improvements from the heart are heard.
1009.C ABCD'S OF KINDNESS

Summary

High interest made this lesson successful. Students enjoy figuring out guidelines and rules.

Creating editorial compliments and critiques based on the teacher's essays is entertaining. Posting the charts of compliments and critiques brings an immediate improvement in the students' writing assignments. Student editors reduce stress and enhance camaraderie.

We now have conversation, collaboration, and camaraderie to keep students aware and involved. How lovely.

> *Get your facts first,*
> *then you can distort them as you please.*
> Mark Twain

1002.E A PLAY BY 2ND GRADERS

The 2nd grade curriculum includes several simple plays. The lesson is based on assigning parts to the students who read them aloud. However, not every child in this class is a good reader. An idea comes to help the nonreaders: If the class writes the play, each student writes their part and is able to read it.

After the class suggests ideas for their play, they vote. Their choice? Use their science unit about dangerous poisons in the house and garage. Two children (the class president and vice president) will tell stories about carelessness and getting in trouble over handling poisons. Lying down for a nap on the stage, they 'dream' the poisons come to life to tell them how to handle poisons properly.

Using the science textbook, each child chooses a poison. Writing their scripts, the children include how the poison is used, what makes it dangerous, and how to be careful with it. As poisons have more than one bad effect, two children can have the same one.

The class is excited! For costumes, we use large brown wrapping paper. A piece twice the child's height is folded in half on the floor. An opening is cut for the head. Taping the sides beneath the child's arms, it becomes a costume.

It is a delightful sight to see the floor covered with paper costumes, and children crawling around drawing and coloring. Putting them on, they look like walking posters. We laugh delightedly and have fun - learning is happening.

Writing his script, one young fellow decides that the family dog will succumb to the gasoline fumes. His mother calls. We talk. Neither of us is able to change his mind. The class says nothing, but no one looks happy when he practices his part and ends with "…and then the dog died."

The class practices twice on the lunch room stage. After the 2nd practice session, the children invite the other classes to be our audience. A few children help the class secretary write an invitation. The office staff makes copies for her. She and the treasurer deliver them to the classrooms. That night, the class takes invitations home to their parents.

The performance
The next day after lunch, 2 kindergartens, 2 first grades, the other 2nd grade, and 2 third grades file into the auditorium. Several parents arrive. We have a full house!

The young performers form a line behind the curtain in order of their presentations. I sit in front near the stage. The 2 'problem children' tell their tales of mishandling poisons. They 'get tired, lie down, and fall asleep' on their pillows.

One by one the actors and actresses step from behind the curtain, tell their concerns about a poison. and give important advice about handling it - while shaking a finger at the sleeping figures. Finishing their parts, the children step back behind the curtain and go to the end of the line.

Our young fellow with the dog changes his mind and explains that the pet dog gets sick licking gasoline and *almost* dies. I breath a thank you. His mother tells me later that she, too, breathed a sigh of relief.

After the applause, the children line up to leave the auditorium. The other 2nd grade teacher stops me and says she is surprised that the children wrote their own play. "But" she says. " I am most amazed that you sit out front and watch the play while the children are behind the curtain without a chaperone." I smile. Being a 2nd

year teacher, I do not even think of chaperones. The children know what to do. I know they know. It is the trust factor.
1010.K THE TRUST FACTOR

Summary
Children love to write and perform plays. As plays cover the 3 learning styles, student interest is highs. The auditory children learn by speaking and listening. Visual learners love drawing and seeing the costumes. This locks in the information for them. Moving around the floor and observing the activities, the kinesthetic children act out new ideas. The AVK class is 100% involved in creating a play.
1005.A FLOOR LETTERS OF RED YARN
1011.H 3 STYLES OF LEARNING – AVK

It is curious as to why the 2nd graders never said a word about the dog story. 7-year-olds seem to have their own way of handling 'outside the norm' behavior. They give it no attention.. It seems, without recognition, a behavior fades away, or at least changes.

Thinking is easy, acting is difficult,
and to put one's thoughts into action
is the most difficult thing
in the world.
Wolfgang van Goethe

1002.F 4 BOYS SUCCEED
Four students are older than their 2nd grade class because they haven't passed grade level reading tests. Held back 2 years means they are 9 years old while their classmates are 7. They are literally head and shoulders above the other children.

The boys' first taste of reading success is helping each other write and practice their lines for the science play. To build on their success, they are given opportunities to write and read their reading assignments as a team of 4. Their reading abilities improve significantly. The new experience of independence and collaboration diminishes their fears of failure.

At the end of the year, their ITBS reading test scores are impressively high. The principal decides to skip them over 3rd grade and go straight into 4th. As our school building is K-3, 2nd grade classmates won't notice their move to the 4-6 building. I'm glad for the boys. They earned it.

Note. Although 'losing a year of curriculum' seems to be unfair, the boys are now confident learners. They will catch up as the spiral curriculum repeats itself at a higher level.

Summary
As a team, the boys individualize their assignments - each one works at his ability level. The 'one room school house effect' happens. Children are helping children to learn, new capabilities are revealed, and assignments are completed successfully.

> *Writing is really a strange experience for someone like me.*
> *Not only because I've never written before, but also because*
> *it seems to me that later on neither*
> *I nor anyone else will be interested in the musings*
> *of a thirteen-year-old schoolgirl.*
> Anne Frank

1002.G STUDENTS 'SEIZE THE DAY'
A teacher from Canada, who is teaching a summer education workshop, describes this event as 'a perfect example' of students being capable of working together.

He and his wife are expecting their 1st child. Mr. Phillips explains his plan to his 6th grade class. "After I get the call that my wife is headed to the hospital, I'll call the office. They will call a sub. Someone from the office will come to the room until the sub arrives. You know the day's agenda. It's on the board. Do your best, behave, be respectful to the substitute."

A day later on his way to work, his wife calls. She is headed to the hospital. Off he goes to join her.

Returning the next day, he notices the assignments are neatly stacked and graded. After his class arrives, he asks, "Who was the sub?" Every face beams. "We were!" A student explains, "You forgot to call the office and ask for a sub. When the day starts and no one comes, we decided to run the day ourselves."

Another student continues. "We took the attendance to the office, went to art class, walked out to recess, and then went to lunch. No one asked where you are. At the end of the day we had finished the assignments, so we graded them."

Mr. Phillips is stunned - a whole day with no adult in sight. Looking around the room at the shining independence-proved faces, he smiles. "Amazing. No one even noticed I was gone." The students clamor, "Tell us about the baby!"

Summary
Although it is startling to think a group of students can go through a day without a teacher, notice that they travel on their own only 4 times - to art, the lunchroom, recess, and then home. Familiar with the daily routine, and no one expecting them to be alone, these 12 year olds prove themselves capable of being self-sufficient.

What fun it must have been to be in charge of themselves and discover that they could perform as adults - even correcting their papers.

*Individual commitment to a group effort - that is what makes
a team work, a company work,
a society work, a civilization work.*
Vince Lombardi

...and a class work. :)

1002.H TO SUCCEED IN SCHOOL

Story
The after school meeting includes the tutoring student's mom, his classroom teacher, and the tutor. None of us understand Howard's problem. Why does it take him forever to finish a writing assignment? Oher school work takes the normal time to complete.

During his tutoring session, he's asked why he takes so long. He answers, "Do you know how many different words can be used in each sentence? I think over every word before I decide the best one." Howard is not a slow writer, he is a deliberate thinker. Hearing about his answer, his teacher allows him to finish written assignments at home.

Story
Throughout her elementary school years, Ellie never finishes a math assignment. Taking them home, they come back unfinished. An adjustment is made. Her math assignment is either the odd problems or even. Able to complete half the work, she happily contributes answers during class discussions. For math tests, only half are assigned and, even if all are correct, the grade is a 'C.' That's okay with both of us.

Eventually, Ellie wants to finish the math assignment at home. Bringing them back completed, her confidence soars. At the parent conference, her mother explains, "It takes Ellie all evening to complete the rest of her math assignment, but she doesn't give up. Finishing her homework is important to her." Over time Ellie's math assignments are completed in class. Her confidence in the classroom led to persistence at home, which led to success.

> *Great things are done by a series*
> *of small things brought together.*
> Vincent Van Gogh

CHAPTER 2 IN CONCLUSION
WE'RE ALL IN THIS TOGETHER!

New information is learned more easily when students work in study teams guided by the teacher. Clear instructions, examples, and detailed procedures help everyone gain confidence. As complex objectives are handled with assurance, stress is significantly reduced. Self-worth is established. Success in teams is carried over to independent work. Knowing how to work with others underpins a successful life.

> *A single conversation with a wise man is better than*
> *ten years study of books.*
> Henry Wadsworth Longfellow

…unless it's a conversation with a butterfly!

Together
Everyone
Achieves
More

Chapter 3
Make it easy to be smart

Achievement on grade level is true success

Topics
A. IQs Go Up   B. Stay on Grade Level   C. Surpass Sameness
D. Spelling Tactics   E. Monotone Test   F. Consider Shyness
G. Indoor Games   H. 20 Questions   I. Solve Mysteries

Introduction

Why make it easy for a student to be smart? If a child is labeled a failure throughout her school career, she needs help desperately and immediately. To begin to defeat the past's disastrous grades, at once assign the child to grade level work - only less. This is the loving thing to do. With shorter assignments, and working with a study partner of similar ability, the child's grades improve. Success is possible.

To establish success for the entire class at the beginning of the school year, assign study partners. Use them to discuss new ideas and for reviews.

Self-individualized assignments allow each student to define a personal goal for accomplishing the required result. The deliberate child adapts the work so there is time to finish. The creatively academic child infuses the assignment with unique ideas. Meeting personal goals on grade level is a given.

This success-based approach rests on "the heart of the child is touched by the love of the teacher, true learning takes place." Responding to the teacher's tender care, students confidently spread their wings for success.

*Success is the sum of small efforts –
repeated day in and day out.*
Robert Collier

1003.A AN IQ CAN GO UP

An IQ is an 'intelligence quotient.' A child takes an IQ test. The test score is compared to other students at the same grade level who take the same test at the same time. A score at the top of the list of scores is considered a high IQ.

However, an unidentified 'glitch' in the ability to read can cause a low IQ score. If the child's low score does not match the child's achievements in the classroom, there is probably a 'glitch.'

High achievers display an extraordinary ability to think logically and creatively. They include,
- Outstanding in a specific area such as sports, music, drawing, or humor.
- An excellent ability to communicate using a large and complex vocabulary.
- An exceptional capacity to solve problems, make decisions, and apply common sense. This is reflected in leadership skills.

An IQ score is negatively impacted by the following glitches.

*Glitch #1 'reading interpretation'
A 1st grader, who participated in discussions above grade level expectations, is not learning to read. Her parents have Annie's verbal ability tested outside the school. She is identified as profoundly gifted, the one in a 250,000 kind. As a new 1st grade teacher, I ask myself, "What does she not understand about the reading process?" My student teacher spends extra time reading to her and pointing out words and letter sounds. We struggle through the year with little success.

In 2nd grade, an experienced teacher recognizes the problem. Annie thinks every syllable she hears is a different word. Nothing on the written page matches her concept of a word. This teacher understands this reading 'glitch.' Thank goodness. Once Annie learns how syllables and words are related, she becomes a successful reader.

*Glitch #2 'write to read'
Three children are 2 years behind in reading. None of the curriculum reading techniques help them. As a school volunteer, a new method is tried. Instead of reading books, the youngsters dictate their own sentences.
1004.A DICTATE TO READ

*Glitch #3 'learn implications'
A 6th grade boy doesn't grasp the underlying process of thinking about reading. Great at decoding words, his understanding is minimal. To answer test questions, he uses the words in the question to find the answer in the paragraph. Learning how to identify implications improves his reading comprehension.
1004.B IMPLICATIONS – THE MILLER

*Glitch #4 'eyes are the problem'
Testing well in the primary grades, Tiffany is placed in the enrichment program. In 4th grade, her reading test scores drop significantly. It's thought that putting her in the advanced program is a mistake. Her complaints about headaches hint that her eyes might be the problem.

An optometrist discovers that one eye starts reading the sentence, then the other eye takes over in a different place. Nothing she reads makes sense. Eye exercises and eyeglasses help her eyes to work together. Regaining her ability to see the words properly, Tiffany's school work returns to its previous level of success.

Summary
If a child displays a keen intelligence yet scores a low IQ, consider checking for reading glitches. Taking the IQ test again and without the glitch, the IQ score may go up.

Consider, too, the effect of team work. A 5th grader, given an opportunity to work in a small group, proves her innate intelligence. Her IQ and national test scores go up. These 2 lessons tell her story.
1003.E A TEST READ IN MONOTONE
1008.G THE ROMAN EMPIRE

Humor improves IQ
Sarah Henderson's March 21, 2015, article on the Internet *Laughter and Learning: Humor Boosts Retention* identifies the role of humor in developing intelligence.

She assesses silly humor as useless whereas content-related humor improves retention. A teacher's wit and dry humor clarifies comprehension. As students relax and anxiety decreases, they pay close attention to the information and remember more. Her article is a worthwhile read.

> *There is little success where there is little laughter.*
> Andrew Carnegie

1003.B STAY ON GRADE LEVEL
Reduce the length of a grade level assignment, and it encourages a failing student to catch-up to the class. It is a great motivator to be able to answer questions during the class discussion.

Story
On the first day of 2nd grade, Shannon walks straight up to me and announces, "This year I'm going to learn to read." At that point,

according to his student information folder, he knows only half the letters of the alphabet and is assigned to the lowest ability reading group.

To reach his goal, he needs specific support because his work load is about to increase. His mom agrees to work with him at home. Unfinished assignments are taken home for help.

To help Shannon progress quickly, he is given assignments outside his reading group. When the 2nd grade reading group meets, he joins them. It's definitely extra work for him to be in 2 reading groups, but he is a very determined lad.

At the end of the school year, Shannon is only a few weeks shy of finishing the 2nd grade reading materials. His resolve and ongoing commitment lead to his success. (K through 2nd in one year!) The 3rd grade teacher agrees to give him extra assignments and double group him until he reaches grade level reading. Congratulations, Shannon!

Story
A 4th grade girl, who is 3 years behind in reading, comes for tutoring. Her mother brings her assignments from the reading specialist. Grace is doing the same worksheets she did in 1st grade. Mom is concerned that her child is giving up. For me, it's amazing she keeps doing them.

Together, we set up an original approach. During tutoring sessions, she is given 4th grade worksheets that her classroom teacher willingly supplies. The sessions focus on 'how to think' about the information.

The classroom teacher agrees that Grace can finish her assignments at home with Mom. The reading specialist at school focuses on understanding the directions for 4th grade assignments. For Grace, grade level work is a great motivator.

Thanks to the specialist, the teacher's efforts, Mom's assistance at home, and tutoring, the youngster improves rapidly. Discovering she is capable of 4th grade work, Grace's reading ability surges upward. All her subjects are favorably impacted. A caring team of adults makes the difference.

Story
Fifth grader George is reading at a 2nd grade level. What happened? George's private school combined classrooms. Having 3 teachers, no one caught on that he had convinced other students to do his work. George's mother decides to homeschool and adds in private tutoring sessions.

Mom purchases homeschool curriculum materials that match George's actual grade level. It's a challenge. Beginning with what he understands, we push forward. For 3 years, George's homeschool curriculum is enriched with critical thinking skills and discussions around high interest information.

George's dream is to attend a private school. He is undaunted. Just before the school year starts, he begins packing. His parents ask the school's admissions officer to call me I say, "I know he can succeed if he's given support during the transition." Support is promised.

The next day, George is accepted. His parents load his suitcases into the car and off they go. During the next 5 years, his love of science gives him the opportunity to join a select group of 6 honor students.

His father expresses gratitude for his son's success. "Without you, this wouldn't have happened," he says. My response is, "Without a son who is willing to work hard and parents to support his high goals, he could not have succeeded."

Summary
The child who completes below grade level worksheets is in a 'catch 22.'

The child learns, but never catches up. (Unless double grouping is used as was with Shannon.)

Shorter grade level assignments, plus a study partner to explain the details, and a desire to succeed, leads the child to success. For the struggling child, sharing an answer during a class lesson is a game changer. The newfound confidence boosts self-worth. And on the youngster goes to higher accomplishments.

> *Nothing in the world can take the place of persistence....*
> *Persistence and determination alone are omnipotent.*
> Calvin Coolidge

1003.C INDIVIDUALIZE TO SURPASS SAMENESS

With a change in school population, my teaching assignment is switched from 5th to 1st grade. The very experienced co-teachers offer to help adjust my expectations for younger children. On the first day of school, they stop by the classroom with a stack of worksheets. The papers represent years of careful collecting. I am impressed. Carefully placing them on the table by the door, they nod, smile, and leave.

Staring in astonishment at the 5 inch stack, I recall my first principal saying, "After you hand out an assignment, correct it, and give it back the next day. Children deserve immediate feedback to find out what to improve." Does this stack of papers represent future evenings filled with correcting worksheets? I am about to find out.

During the first week, the 1st graders finish worksheets almost faster than they are handed out. Why? Because the directions are simple, the worksheets seldom require much effort to complete. They range from practice in writing letters to tracing math numbers to connecting the dots for seasonal pictures. From coloring to cut outs - every type of activity imaginable awaits the students.

Directions include,
- Put a letter in the blank.
- Circle the letter sound to match the picture.
- Put an 'X' on the picture that doesn't fit.
- Trace the word.
- Color the right answer red.
- Put a check by….

Evenings are busy checking and drawing red stars on their papers. The students have them back the next day. I wonder. In 5th grade, students have assignments that require time to complete. Are the 1st graders capable of doing longer assignments? An idea pops. Let them create individualized worksheets that take more time.

Example
A typical 1st grade math worksheet shows a circle in different sizes with a color word inside each. "Color the circle to match the color word." Whoosh. Finished in a flash! Asking for neat coloring slows no one down. They must have learned accuracy and speed in Kindergarten. A new approach is developed.

An 'individualized' geometry assignment starts with a blank sheet of paper, pencil, and crayons. First, 4 geometric shapes are drawn on the board. The shapes' names are listed to the right. As the children identify what makes the shapes different or the same, lines are drawn between the word and its shape.

Next the individualized assignment is explained. "Draw the shapes in any size on your paper. Write the correct label next to it. On the back, choose at least 2 shapes to make an animal. Fill in the animal shapes with solid colors or designs - stripes, bubbles, or even waves."

As the freedom to personalize ideas is a new concept, an example is drawn on the board. A dazzling combination of shapes, colors, and designs form an imaginary animal. Children unsure of creating an individualized animal are encouraged to copy this one. The class starts drawing. As creative thinking takes longer, there is time to teach reading groups.

Later, the students describe the shapes used to make their animals. The children spontaneously clap and praise each other. It's their celebration of success. Grading the papers with a red star and returning them the next day is fast and easy. The success of this individualized assignment leads to revising other curriculum assignments.

The 1st grade co-teachers? After 2 weeks, they notice their stacks of worksheets are untouched and no more are left. Perhaps they see the children's individualized assignments posted in the hallway.

*Vocabulary and themes
Middle school tutoring students often bring a list of vocabulary words with instructions to write a sentence for each word. They struggle to think of sentence ideas until a theme is identified. Asking, "What's a place or thing you know well?" answers range from a sport, a hobby, their yard, to the school lunchroom. With a theme, it's easier to choose a detail, add the vocabulary word, and create a sentence.

For instance, solar system vocabulary is combined with lunchroom details. The sentences reflect an understanding of the meanings.

- The bright <u>moon</u> shines on the white napkin.
- His serving of mashed potatoes could cover the <u>planet</u> Jupiter.
- A friend <u>orbits</u> the table twice before sitting down.
- My green broccoli fell toward the <u>earth</u> and onto the floor.

Reason morphs. Creativity pops. Sentence writing 'self-adjusts' to the student's ability. It's easy to be smart – it's joyful.

*Vocabulary + a definition
A vocabulary sentence may require the word and part of its definition. With the student's theme, the activity is individualized. Taking longer to do, fewer words are assigned, and fewer sentences need correcting.

Directions
"For each word, look up its definitions, and choose one.
Combine the word and the definition to write an original sentence. Use your theme. Underline the word and its definition."

Example
Theme. a lake
Vocabulary word: map. Definition: the land's surface.
Sentence. When I got lost in the woods, my <u>map</u> showed me the <u>land's surface</u> around the lake.

Summary
Based on an individualized approach to interpret assignments, student learning becomes interesting, personal, and doable. Eventually, the students incorporate their own creative twists into their assignments. Team work provides creativity and a support system.

Benefits of individualized assignments
- Students don't need to copy. Looking at another paper only jump starts an idea.
- Academic understanding is enriched by individualized thinking - reason morphs and creative interpretations pop! Students invest more time and effort because stress is reduced.
- As their ideas are shared with the class, confidence and recall improve.

For the teacher? Correcting these worksheets is easy and fast. The children will have them back the next day.
1005.K Grade Writing Assignments Fast

No amount of skillful invention can replace
the essential element of imagination.
Edward Hopper

1003.D SPELLING TACTICS

Story

In 9th grade, my math teacher didn't accept a correct math
answer. Instead of the word 'pound,' the symbol # was used.
She explained that # also meant 'number.' Telling her that my mother
used the symbol on her grocery list fell on deaf ears. Who would have
guessed a math teacher cared enough about a math symbol, to mark an
answer wrong?

Questions

Should misspelled words, including symbols and abbreviations, affect a
right answer and the grade? Is student creativity compromised by taking
time to identify and apply correct spelling? Does anyone care about
spelling? Does spellcheck make correct spelling a moot point?

What makes spelling important?

    a. Spelling words incorrectly locks the wrong spelling into long term
memory.

    b. Spelling makes a difference in reading the ITBS test or filling out
a job application.

    c. Correct spelling demands analytical thinking which improves
intelligence.

    d. Misspelled words make the writer appear ill-informed and
uneducated.

    e. In today's tech world, spell-check may bring up a 'similar, yet
incorrect word,' which changes the meaning of the sentence. For
instance, typing 'ster' spellcheck chooses 'stir' instead of 'star.'
"Check out the sky! There are millions of stirs tonight!"

It's best to know the correct spelling of a word.

Grading student spelling
When it's easy for students to spell the words correctly, then spelling counts as part of the grade. The following tactics are proven successful. Writing speed and creativity combine

Spelling Tactics

Word chart
In a 1st grade classroom, a 6 foot wide chart of alphabetized basic spelling words is posted high on the wall. As a review, the teacher holds up a long stick and asks, "Who wants to read the words?" Hands wave! The teacher chooses a student who comes forward, takes the stick, points to the first word, and reads it aloud. Continuing down the list, he stops when a word is missed. The stick is then handed to another waving hand. It is mesmerizing to watch the stick go from word to word. With the basic words in plain sight, spelling them correctly is easy and required.

Shout out!
When this class of 1st graders needs a word spelled, they call it out. Usually another student spells it, but if no one does, the teacher spells it aloud and writes it on the board. The children are not distracted as they continue to write. A unique method to be sure, and it works.

Brainstorm a word list
Before the writing assignment begins, the class identifies vocabulary words related to the topic. Written on the board, the words serve 2 purposes - correct spelling and ideas for the writing activity. Asked for a word during the assignment, the teacher adds it to the board.

Notebook theme lists
At the top of a notebook page, students record the writing theme and date. As the class brainstorms relevant vocabulary words, they are written on the board. Afterwards, the students copy the words into their notebook. With a focused activity, correct spelling happens.

Alphabetized pages
Copying words into a notebook with one page for each letter didn't work. Most students don't take the time to look up a word. Dictionaries aren't used either. Why? It's difficult to look up a word without knowing the first few letters. For me, by the time the first 3 letters are given, the whole word might as well be written on the board.

Good spellers help others
Some students are naturally great spellers. Sometimes, the talented speller is asked to review another student's work and correct the spelling. The 'student proofreader' signs his/her name at the bottom of the page. This technique is used for *final proofing*.

Pencil circles and blank spaces
The student makes a light circle around a word that 'probably needs to be fixed.' Walking around the room, the teacher lightly pencils the correct spelling in the margin. After the word is fixed, the margin word is erased. Or the student writes the first letter and leaves a blank space. Again, the teacher provides the word. Note. If writing on the paper proves too distracting for the student, write the word on the board.

Spelling Bees
This game encourages students to practice spelling words from social studies, science, and math. As an option for the Bee, have the child and a partner write the word on the board.
1001.G An Answer Poem

Story

A 6th grade boy is tutored to improve his spelling. No matter what spelling technique is taught, John's spelling does not improve. At one of his tutoring sessions, he's asked, "Why isn't your spelling improving?" He answers, "Why bother? I've learned them wrong, and it's too hard to learn them over. Plus, no one at school cares."

Touché. From then on, his sentences are observed as he writes them. A spelling mistake is written correctly on the board, and he copies it 3 times on the board, then fixes his paper. He very quickly starts to catch his mistakes and corrects them before they are written on the board. It's a giant step toward self-correcting. Somebody cares.

Story

A co-teacher relates this experience from the 1970's. In her 2nd grade classroom is a boy who has been held back repeatedly because he can't read or write. Being a 12 year old grouped with 7 year old children, Eddie's failure is obvious.

One bright classmate asks if she can teach him the spelling lists. Permission is granted providing her classwork is perfect. (She tends to rush through her assignments which results in careless mistakes.)

As the weeks go by, the older youngster passes his spelling tests. To celebrate Eddie's first 100%, the teacher gives the class a cookie party. This is a game changer for him and the class. The other children begin to encourage him. As success breeds confidence, Eddie makes an effort to read and write. His academic work improves dramatically.

When Eddie's progress is shared with the principal, she tests him thoroughly - in fact, all afternoon. With results in hand, she moves him to a 4th grade classroom. This is a true story. Hooray for the authentic one room school house approach - children helping children. Kudos to Eddie for his willingness to learn.

Summary

It's easier to spell accurately when words are at hand. As ideas pour through the pencil to the paper, proper spelling makes it easier to write accurately. Yes, in today's classroom, correct spelling can count toward the grade.

My spelling is Wobbly. It's good spelling but it Wobbles,
and the letters get in the wrong places.
A.A. Milne

1003.E A TEST READ IN MONOTONE

Taffy's IQ is just high enough for her to be in a regular classroom. Her self-image and desire to succeed change dramatically during the 2nd semester when the class votes to present a play about the Roman Empire. 1008.G THE ROMAN EMPIRE

With her team's support, Taffy writes her script and acts her part. This is a huge step for a child who seldom participates. Most important, she watches the other skits attentively. She gains confidence and knowledge. Her self-worth improves.

On the day of the final test, it becomes clear that Taffy's low reading level is being tested not her knowledge of the Roman Empire. For me, it's essential for her to prove what she has learned. After the tests are handed out, I tell the class, "I'll be reading the test aloud to Taffy in a monotone voice. She will mark her answers on the answer sheet. By using a monotone, the questions and answers will not be emphasized in any way."

Taffy and I stand at the front of the room with Taffy's back to the class. I read aloud quietly. A stillness comes over the students. They are following along! When Taffy turns around and realizes what is happening, she smiles happily. Her classmates are proving their support as they join her in taking the test.

Taffy's Roman Empire test grade is a solid 'B.' She is thrilled. Her confidence takes off. For the rest of the year, she participates fully in her 'reading book club.' It's a red letter day when her original poem is videotaped.

At the end of the year, Taffy's ITBS scores reflect her self-confidence and improved reading ability. Instead of progressing one year or less, her progress is almost 2 full years. Understanding how questions and answers relate plus the support of her fellow classmates, contributes to her success. When the heart of this child is touched by her caring classmates, her success happens.

Summary
Reading a test in a monotone voice to a poor reader is a small adjustment to be sure. However, when a low reading level causes low grades in other subjects, reading a test aloud gives the child an opportunity to find out that they are smart. As the child's confidence builds, reading on grade level happens.

> *Nothing can stop the individual*
> *with the right mental attitude from achieving a goal.*
> *Nothing on earth can help the individual*
> *with the wrong mental attitude.*
> Thomas Jefferson.

1003.F Shy Child

Abby ducks her head when it's time to present her report to the class. Panic brings the 5th grader almost to tears. To lessen her fear, she's told to ask some friends to come to the classroom after eating lunch. As they sit on the floor, Abby sits in a chair facing them and reads her report.

It is a small event compared to the students who stand before a class of 29 pairs of eyes to present their reports. Yet, it develops her confidence in speaking in front of others. Her grade is not affected. Her friends are delighted to help.

Summary
Even adults may panic at the thought of standing before a group. A thoughtful and compassionate response allows a child to earn a grade for an oral report, and take a step toward conquering fear.

1003.G GAMES FOR INDOOR RECESS
Indoor recess games improve analysis and evaluation levels of thinking. It takes effective strategies to win. Better thinking translates to better learning.

*Connect the Dots
Using a grid of 10 dots by 10 dots, the first player draws a line to connect 2 dots. The 2nd player does the same. The goal is twofold. Complete a square, and block the other player's moves. Initials are put in a completed box, and another turn is taken. It gets wild toward the end when one player, having made a box, completes another one nearby and keeps going.

Note. Using one inch graph paper, makes it easier to draw the dots.
Note. A game not finished at the end of recess can be saved until the next day.

*Puzzles
Strategies include *fill in the corners and outside edges first; *gather similar colors; *arrange clusters according to the picture on the box. Strategic thinking improves the ability to solve real life problems.

Summary
Games make it fun to be smart! From puzzles to checkers to chess, all require rules and strategies to win. Thinking improves as students,
- Plan their moves ahead.
- Guess the other player's next move.
- Analyze the implications of the rules.
- Evaluate how to play the game better next time.

> *Man is most nearly himself when he achieves*
> *the seriousness of a child at play.*
> Heraclitus

1003.H TWENTY QUESTIONS. TERRIFIC THINKERS!

The teacher begins the game.
"I'm thinking of an object in this room. All of you can see it. You have 20 questions with 'yes' 'no' answers to guess the object. I'll keep track of the questions on the board." 20 dots are drawn on the board.

For each question - "Is it the flag? Is it the door? Is it the light?" - a dot is erased. Quickly, the game is over. They lose. The object is pointed out. A class discussion follows.

STUDENTS "There are too many objects to guess, 20 questions aren't enough."
TEACHER "What other kinds of questions can you ask?"
STUDENTS "We can ask the color."
The teacher chooses another object; the class plays again. 'Is it red? Blue?" White? Yellow?" The 20 dots quickly disappear.

STUDENTS "Maybe we should ask about the size, too."
They play again asking color and size questions. Poof. The 20 dots are gone.
STUDENTS "Maybe we should ask where it is."
 "Is it on a table? Is it near the door?" They soon ran out of dots.

The children are now immersed in thinking strategies. Their questions and answers begin to connect as though running up and down a spider web of dew drops to find a pattern. Analysis and evaluation of their strategies come together.

Beginning again, the first question is 'location specific.' "Is it in the front of the room?" Like a funnel, the questions take off. "Is it above the table?" "Is it in the corner?" When the location is clear, the questions focus on color and size. Success! The object is identified. Over time, the class defines what is meant by location. Sometimes a child runs around part of the room to point out the area described.

The class learns to pay attention to the 'no' answer. If "Is the object in the back of the room?" is answered 'no,' then it is in the front. Color words develop into attribute words - striped, fuzzy, smooth, dark, lightweight. When how to the game is understood, the students take turns being the leader.

Summary
Games create thinkers and philosophers. Playing strategy games is essential to education.

Story
A 5th grade student thinks like an adult. She asks unique questions and tackles difficult assignments using strategies beyond the other students' capabilities. Her methods reflect more than a high IQ.

Asked, "Why is your thinking so different from the other students?" Kristie explains, "When my brother and I were little, our dad got mad because we watched so much TV. He took it outside and broke it into pieces. After that, we invented our own entertainment.

We write and put on plays, and build projects. I can do things for myself." The effects of removing technology from young children's lives is obvious. An *individualized life style* leads to independent and capable children.

Question. Did the one room school house of K-8 students which had no technology, graduate students at the same thinking level as today's high school students?

The power to question is the basis of all human progress.
Indira Gandhi

1003.I SOLVE MINI-MYSTERIES
Playing 20 Questions, the students' strategic thinking is tested further by solving mysteries.

Mystery
An avalanche roars down the mountainside. Rescuers ski to a house they know is in its path. The house is still standing. The fireplace blazes brightly. A candle on the table is burning. The room is empty. The family is obviously gone. What happened and why?

Ask questions
It is suggested to the class that their questions begin with the scene's details. For example, "Is the door open? Is the avalanche close to the house?" Confirming and clarifying the broader facts help interpret details.

Note. If a question is asked, "Is the door is open?" it needs to define whether 'open' means 'unlocked' or is 'opened wide.'

Note. If the question has no relevance such as, "What color is the house?," the 'answer dot' is labeled 'NA' - 'Not Applicable' and is not erased.

Summary
The Encyclopedia Brown mysteries are the class favorites. In essence,

there is always a small, every day fact that Leroy Brown notices, and no one else does. That fact solves the mystery.

Note. Asking broad then detailed questions is the key to solving mysteries.
Note. An Internet search for 'mini mystery stories for 20 questions' identifies several books.

> *We get wise by asking questions.*
> *And even if they are not answered, we get wise.*
> *For a well-packed question carries its answer on its back*
> *as a snail carries its shell.*
> James Stephens

CHAPTER 3 IN CONCLUSION
MAKE IT EASY TO BE SMART

'Make it easy to be smart' does not mean students are no longer responsible for learning. Nor does it leave the learner with an insignificant education. 'Make it easy' is not working below grade level. It is not having someone else do the work.

'Make it easy to be smart' provides new opportunities for children to accomplish grade level work. Study teams based on similar abilities give deliberate students support and time to finish their work. This careful and deep thinking 'locks in information.' Designing self-individualized assignments challenges the high level learners to embellish and elaborate the assignment.

As each component of a unique assignment is analyzed and transformed, creativity pops and academics morph to new levels of accomplishment. All children are smart when the teacher makes it easy to be smart!

The direction in which education starts a man
will determine his future in life.
Plato

PART II

The Subjects

Chapter 4 Reflect on Reading

Chapter 5 Consider Writing

Chapter 6 Discover Math

Chapter 7 Investigate Science

**Chapter 8 A Foundation for Culture:
Social Studies and History**

Chapter 4
Reflect on Reading

Make inferences, prove understanding

Topics
A. Dictate To Read   B. Identify Implications   C. Validate Facts
D. Memorize Poems   E. Dr. Seuss   F. Stages of Reading
G. Phases of Reading   H. Reading Glitches

Introduction
A reader enters into the thoughts of the writer. Books, articles, essays, quotations, and poems, unique subjects, inspirational ideas, and entertaining stories become, for a little while, one's own views. As an alert reader, children must consider the impact of the writer's outlooks. "Should these thoughts be mine?" Examine and compare them to one's personal belief system. "Am I enriching my understanding or changing it drastically?" By this process, the child gains useful knowledge, wisdom, and common sense.

An author's concept of time, space, and place interprets, explains, and impacts today's world. These words may transform a child from a sheep to a lion or a lion to a sheep.

In the classroom, enrich and expand the students' reading development by reading aloud from a variety of sources. The spoken word reveals the unspoken drama while building vocabulary and improving the listener's ability to hear an entire message without struggling to read new words. Class discussions and questions reveal the implications hidden beneath the surface of an author's words.

Reading accurately is a prized skill. Learned through teacher-led lessons and team collaboration, it impacts students' lives forever.

The reading of all good books is like a conversation
with the finest minds of past centuries.
Rene Descartes

1004.A DICTATE TO READ

New to the community, volunteering at the local elementary school
seems like a good idea. The reading specialist gives me 3 children who
are in 1st grade yet belong in 3rd. As we turn to a page in a simple book,
their faces go blank. Vocabulary flash cards have the same effect. It's
obvious they have given up.

Recalling Sylvia Warner's book about Maori children, who dictate the
words they want to read, a question is asked, Can these children read
sentences that they dictate? Asking them to tell about their favorite
things, one child describes cowboys, another her pet cat, and the third
tells about playing outside.

Asked for his sentence, the cowboy child says, "Cowboys ride their
horses across the range out West." His ability to communicate is beyond
simple words.

Using an 18 inch strip of cardstock, I write his sentence with a black
marker. For each word and punctuation mark, the writing process is
explained.

"Cowboys' is the first word in the sentence, so it needs a capital letter
'C'." It's a compound word made from 'cow' and 'boy.'
"The word 'ride' has a long 'i' sound, so it ends with a silent 'e.'
"The word 'the' is a word put in front of a name word. It's spelled t-h-e."
This detailed analysis combines the grammar basics with the reading
process. The other 2 children listen intently.

As each child's sentence is written, every word, letter, and punctuation mark is cherished as special. At the end of the session, 3 sentence strips are complete. The children are excited to read their own writing.

The next day, the 3 rush into the room and immediately practice their sentences. They are delighted to discover they can read each other's sentences. As words are pointed to, the children read them. Each child dictates another sentence. The detailed analysis connects their spoken words to written ones.

The reading specialist is glad to see the youngsters reading and immediately provides high interest books at their reading level. The reading block is gone. The children are thrilled.

Summary
These 3 youngsters now understand that a book is 'someone's spoken words' on paper. Realizing that the word patterns they use when speaking predicts the next word when reading, the world of books opens up. As we read and discuss what authors think then write, their reading skills and comprehension blossoms! Thank you, Sylvia. A personalized approach provides the encouragement to learn.
1003.C Individualize To Surpass Sameness
1005.B Vocabulary from New Zealand

I have never known any distress
that an hour's reading did not relieve.
Montesquieu

1004.B Implications - The Miller

The new tutoring student stomps into the office yelling, "I can so read!" His mother explains that although Rob is a 7th grader in age, he needs to repeat 6th grade because the school district says his reading scores are seriously below grade level. He sits down folding his arms.

After Mom leaves, Rob is handed a book of fables written at the 7th grade level (Handing him a 'little kids book' adds insult to injury.) Asked to read the first page aloud, he begins, "A long time ago there is an old miller who is very poor."

TEACHER "Stop. Why do you suppose he is poor?"
ROB "I don't know. It doesn't say."
TEACHER "True. So let's analyze what the sentence is telling us. First, the miller is old, which means he's experienced. He must be doing good work, or he'd have no customers and closed the mill a long time ago."
The young man sits up straight. "I didn't think of all that."

TEACHER "What does being poor mean?"
ROB "He doesn't have enough money to buy what he needs like clothes and food."
TEACHER "Exactly. How can he be poor with his experience and customers? A serious problem is suggested in the first sentence, 'Why is the old miller poor?'"

Listening intently, Rob sits taller. It's suggested that the miller's accountant needs glasses and is making mistakes. Rob nods and suggests that the miller needs to raise his prices. For the next hour, we brainstorm ideas and laugh - a sure sign of intelligence and creative thinking.
Our answers are similar to these.

- Perhaps the machinery is broken down, and he's waiting for it to be fixed. Or, maybe it can't be fixed as it's old.
- Perhaps he has a wife who spends more than he makes on clothes, fun with friends, and eating out.
- Perhaps he has older children, and he has to support them.
- Perhaps the farmers owe him money and aren't paying.
- Perhaps he forgets when he takes money from the safe.
- Perhaps he is thinking of retiring and not accepting all the work that comes his way.

- Perhaps a new mill is built nearby, and the farmers are going there because the new machinery is faster and better.
- Perhaps his son is taking over the mill, and he spills a lot of wheat ,so there are fewer bags and less money.
- Perhaps rats get into the bags of wheat. Customers don't like it and go somewhere else.
- Perhaps there is a drought, and the farmers have less wheat to bring him. With less wheat, there is less flour making and less income.

After our 2nd session, his classroom teacher calls his mother and asks what is happening. "Your son's hand is always in the air with answers and questions," she reports. Rob is learning that reading goes beyond decoding words. It includes questioning the obvious and identifying implications.

Summary
Implications explain 'the why' behind the facts. Being able to identify them leads to becoming a better reader.

As to humor and laughter, the Internet provides many articles that define the connection between intelligence, creativity, and humor. The child who disrupts the class with humor may be exceptionally smart.

Note. This is an observation, not an excuse for such behavior. :)

> *There is creative reading as well as*
> *creative writing.*
> Ralph Waldo Emerson

1004.C VALIDATE FACTS
Half of the teachers in the workshop are sitting in a circle. Each one holds a copy of *Jack and Beanstalk*. The other half are sitting outside the inner circle holding their copies. They are the observers for Round One. The first questions are basic. "Is Jack poor? How do you know? "

The real challenge begins when questions go 'outside the box.'
"Is Jack, who accuses the giant of being a thief, in fact a thief and liar himself?"

By the end of the workshop, it is clear that validation is needed to prove a correct answer. Intensive practice has us ready to challenge our Monday morning reading groups with a reading validation technique.

For me, this workshop suggests that the validation process belongs in every subject. My 4th graders are about to be challenged to think harder.

In math. Can you prove that? Who can give another example? Who agrees with that answer? Why? Can the math process be illustrated on the board? How?

In social studies. At what point did the situation change for the soldiers? Find examples in the textbook. How do these events impact battle strategies? Are there other choices? Why does the King think it is right to tax the colonists? Why do the colonists disagree? Validate your answer with facts in the textbook.

Summary
With this 'question and validation' technique, the students find the typical classroom lesson is more interesting. Probing for further information and demanding proof for the answers, keeps students on task and thinking. To introduce this technique, study teams collaborate on the answers.

> *A teacher who is attempting to teach without*
> *inspiring his pupil with a desire to learn*
> *is hammering on cold iron.*
> Horace Mann

1004.D MEMORIZE A POEM

Delighted laughter bursts out as a Shel Silverstein poem is read from his book "A Light In the Attic."

"In everybody's nose
There lives a sharp toothed snail. ..."

Children hoot as they hear the effects of the snail's teeth inside a nose. They laugh again when they see the illustrations. Silverstein's poetry is highly entertaining.

For the assignment, the students copy a favorite poem to be memorized at home. They have 2 weeks in which to recite their poem to the teacher.

Reciting the poem happens as the class walks down the hall to another class or lunch. Handing a copy to the teacher, it is said from memory without help. Grades are A+ A   B+ B
A+ means no mistakes. One mistake A; two a B+. and three is a B. If there are more than 3 mistakes, the child is given another opportunity or chooses another poem.

Summary
The goal is confidence in memorizing. Studying for tests and learning steps to writing or solving math problems is easier when basic information is memorized. Silverstein's humor and creativity is a light moment in the curriculum.

Yesterday is but today's memory, and tomorrow
is today's dream.
Khalil Gibran

1004.E DR. SEUSS REVISITED

Winter break is one week away. The 5th graders are finishing the reading unit. To begin the next one now and continue after the break might be a waste of time. Does anyone recall anything taught 2 weeks ago?

Walking past the library, rolling bookshelf is spotted stuffed with Dr. Seuss books. Is this the answer for next week's reading lessons? Seuss embeds a message or moral in his stories. Reading his books are fun as well as instructive.

After lunch, the class's full attention is on the bookshelf in the front of the room. Will next week be an easy week in reading? Telling them that because these books are golden and not easily replaced, they will not be taken home. Their smiles widen. Dr. Seuss *and* no reading homework.

Each student chooses a book. On an index card, they write the book title and their name. After reading the book, they write 3 questions, The index card is placed in the book. Only that student - the Book Checker - knows the answers.

To provide authenticity to the reading activity, each student is given a personalized record sheet for their book answers. Their *best handwriting* is required as this activity is important work.

Dr. Seuss Record Sheet

Name_____

Title   Answers   Score

It's time to read Seuss books. Questions are answered, then checked. Scores are given to the Dr. Seuss Master Record Keeper, the teacher. Using Dr. Suess books, reading success is guaranteed for every child.

A chart lists the alphabetized book titles and the initials of the Book Checkers. Spaces to the right are for the reader's initials and a smiley face sticker. No scores are posted.

Note. Because the librarian's check out list shows the books in alphabetical order, it is easy to make the chart.

The teacher's job is keeping track of who reads what, scores, and handing out smiley faces. No papers to grade as the students are in charge. The reader of the book and Book Checker figure out any discrepancies about the answers.

At the end of the day's reading session, we discuss Dr. Seuss's 'embedded messages.' From the environment to safety, he always says something. It's a delightful week revisiting Dr. Seuss. The students apply insight and understanding to something they know well.

After winter break
When the 2nd semester begins, Book Clubs based on specific authors or topics replace the standard reading groups. The Great Brain series by John Dennis Fitzgerald challenges the better readers. Their questions discuss characters, events, and compare time lines.

The Nature Poetry Club is assigned a variety of poems and poets. Analyzing and evaluating a poem's different meanings challenges the students' thinking. Comparing and contrasting poems about similar topics provides analysis questions.

Story
One day, an advanced reader complains about his assignments.
 "I want to be in the easy book club."
"Fine," I tell him. "As long as you are busy with the assignments from Monday through Friday." He's done by Wednesday. Deciding the poetry

club isn't as interesting as he thought, he resumes reading the Great
Brain books and catches up with his assignments.

Summary
Dr. Seuss provides entertainment and high level thinking skills.
Choosing which books to read, everyone is committed. Discussing Dr.
Seuss's messages makes the last week before vacation a busy one. These
2 articles describe question techniques.
1011.E THINK SMARTER WITH BLOOM 1,2,3
1011.F THINK SMARTER WITH BLOOM 4,5,6

Dr. Carson
World renowned brain surgeon Dr. Ben Carson learns the importance of
reading in the elementary grades. Falling behind in his assignments, he
gives up. With 3 jobs from 5 a.m. to midnight, his mother has no time to
help him read books. She sends him to the library where the librarian
helps him and his brother choose books.

Mom's follow up questions about his challenging books means he must
read carefully and thoughtfully. In a year and a half, his grades soar. He
wins an award for Best Student. In high school, Dr. Carson graduates at
the top of his class. Mom's interest, encouragement, and belief that her
son is capable of reading well makes the difference.

Note. Mom's questions are based on her curiosity and ability to identify
implications.

> *If one cannot enjoy reading a book over and over again,*
> *there is no use in reading it at all.*
> Oscar Wilde

1004.F READING STAGES
Each stage of reading is applied to learning new information. The
reading process begins with new vocabulary and ends with implications.

As children are challenged by higher levels of reading, their vocabulary and comprehension increases. Yet, an easy reading book on an interesting topic is still to be cherished!

Story
The 2nd grader enters the tutoring office clasping a popular middle school novel. Her mother explains, "Her brother is reading this book, and she wants to read it, too. Please help her out." Mom turns and leaves. The young girl smiles happily.

Dutifully, we open the book. Reading the first sentence, 3 words are unfamiliar .Pausing, she sounds them out. Decoding done, she asks, "What do they mean?" I explain. After a few minutes of 'stop, decode, explain, continue' it is clear the youngster is losing track of the story line. Asked why she wants to read this book, she replies that her brother describes its exciting adventures, and she wants to read the details on her own.

We try a new tactic. She listens while I read a paragraph and pause to explain vocabulary and the story line. It is now plain to me that if a 2nd grade reading level of *Harry Potter* is written, it will be a best seller. This youngster truly wants to read this book.

When Mom returns, she agrees to read the book aloud, then explain the story. It's now a Cliff Notes' interpretation. Despite this youngster's enthusiasm, the book is too difficult. She has not reached that stage of reading.

DEFINITION
Stage. An advancing degree of progression. For example, the stages of a plant's growth.   Noah Webster's 1828 Dictionary

Based on observations of student reading, 7 specific stages of reading take place when new material is introduced. From memorized words to finding content clues, children apply specific skills as reading becomes more complex.

These 7 stages repeat whenever new information is read. For instance, a text book either explains the chapter's new vocabulary before students read the information, or the teacher gives a list of words to look up. The first 3 reading stages are based on *learning vocabulary* while the last 4 are based on *reading techniques*.

PART I
3 stages based on techniques to build vocabulary

Stage 1. *Memorization… repeat the words.*

Hearing a simple story several times, a young child soon memorizes the words. Turning the pages, the little one happily chants the story. To improve the child's memory, read the story out loud in a lyrical voice. By including an expressive interpretation, its drama increases long term memory.

Stage 2. *Sight Words… immediate word recognition*

Recognizing specific words and their derivatives (roll, rolls, rolling) increases reading level. As the child chants the words, point to the specific words. This builds a collection of sight words. Writing them on index cards lets the child practice them until they are automatically recognized.

Note. To differentiate reading sight words from 'memory chanting,' observe the child's eyes. Are they moving across the page as they read the words?

Stage 3a. *Decode… with letter sounds*

Decoding the sounds of the alphabet letters usually produces the word. (The sound of a letter is not the same as its name.) Because the American language includes words from around the world; these letter sounds are not consistent. Words such as 'eight' and 'ate,' 'fish' and 'phone' have similar sounds and different spellings.

Decoding rules are specifically taught. For instance, an 'e' at the end of the word, means the vowel one consonant before it has a long sound. (rip becomes ripe) 'gh' has the same impact (lit becomes light).

Stage 3b. *Decode… with syllables*

The pronunciation of a new word is also based on familiar syllables. For instance, tele-phone, tele-graph and tele-vision help to decode the word telekinetic. Decoding is a lifelong process. I recall my surprise when the word 'drought' is not spelled 'drout!'

PART II
4 stages based on techniques to build comprehension

Stage 4. *Analyze* … *find clues to a word's meaning*

To learn this technique, student teams examine the paragraph for definition clues to a new word. For instance, the word 'abatement' may be near the word 'reduce' in the next sentence. Or there is a description of something slowing down such as a car approaching a red light.

A well-written grade level book provides clues that define new vocabulary.

Stage 5. *Visualize… mentally 'see' the story*

This has two applications.

First, some readers mentally 'see' where a word is located on the page. Skimming the pages quickly, the word is soon found.

Second, the reader creates an 'internal movie.' Linking sentences to mental pictures develops comprehension, improves recall, and clarifies interpretation. This is a good skill to have.

Activity
To learn 'mental seeing,' students illustrate a sentence from the story or textbook and add original details that fit the information. As students share their pictures and interpretations, the story events and characters are better understood and remembered.

For instance, drawing Cinderella sitting by the fireplace scrubbing the stones, may show her dirty dress, ashes scattered about, and a wisp of smoke rising from the embers. Now that makes a mental image!

Note. For young children, the book's illustrations develop the ability 'to see' a story. Explain the illustration, so they recall story details later.

Stage 6. *Connect ideas… * *from today to the past or other sources*

Linking new information to known facts makes it easier to recall a new word or fact.

Before telling an unfamiliar story, establish an information base. For instance, an unfamiliar story such as "Little Toot," who lives in a NYC harbor, benefits from illustrations of the harbor and a discussion of ships. It's rather like a movie trailer.
1005.F THIRD GRADERS. FIRST TIME WRITERS

Stage 7. *Identify implications… * *recognize effects and causes.*

A deep analysis identifies 'possible effects and causes' of events and characters' behaviors. This is technique is specifically taught.
1004.B IMPLICATIONS – THE MILLER

Efficient reading
A key characteristic of good reading is 'mentally seeing' the information as though a movie is playing. A less able reader decodes the words, but without the 'movie technique' does not fully grasp the interactions between the details.

Story
A 1st grader exhibits a keen ability to 'see' a story event. The story in his reading group is about 4 race cars. The yellow car is determined to win the race at any cost. Ahead of the other cars, he throws a box on the road. The car behind him runs over the box and gets stuck. Next, he throws tacks on the road. The next car behind him runs over the tacks and blows out its tires. The last car speeds forward, passes the yellow car, and wins the race. The children clap and cheer. The 'mean yellow car' does not win.

Our young lad asks, "Aren't the tacks still on the road? Why doesn't the last car run over the tacks and blow out its tires?" He 'saw' the story in his head and caught the obvious. The children discuss his question and decide that all the tacks are picked up by the second car's tires. Whew. Creative reasoning saves the day in answering an observant question. (Our editor Bruce suggests self-sealing tires prevented tacks from blowing out the tires. He is a great first grade thinker.)

At conference time, the boy's mother expresses her concern that her son is in the lowest reading group. "Don't worry," I tell her. "He's the best thinker in the class. Deliberate, careful thinking slows down the reading process." The 'deliberate' writer is described in this article.
1009.E IDENTIFY STUDY teams

Summary

When reading materials are new, the 7 stages begin again from sight words and decoding words to analyzing and recognizing implications.

*To build vocabulary, a child -
1. Memorizes the story, and then points to the words.
2. Learns sight words through practice.
3. Decodes with letter sounds and/or with syllables.

*To build comprehension, a child -
4. Analyzes the paragraph for clues to a definition.
5. Visualizes the story information.
6. Connects new ideas to familiar ones.
7. Identifies implications.

A book written for a specific grade level means it contains words, grammar, and ideas specific to the child's age. To figure out a book's reading level, there are several tests online.

Without continual growth and progress, such words as improvement, achievement, and success have no meaning.
Benjamin Franklin

1004.G PHASES OF READING - from easy to hard.

Is the book too easy? Too hard? Just right? Each reading phase plays a specific role for the reader. Children who read books at many phases build a variety of skills.

An 'easy to read book today' develops the skills that support tomorrow's challenging book. Note. The following 5 phases and explanations are based on personal observations.

Phase 1. *Reads far below ability level.*

Reading aloud, the words fly out of a child's mouth quickly as decoding happens within a momentary pause. As grammar and vocabulary are familiar, the information is understood .This reading material is definitely *below* the child's ability to read. However, what if this level is all that the child wants to read?

Encourage more reading based on different topics. For instance, microscopes are explained at the first grade level and fifth.
Am important fact. Speed reading improves when there is no challenge to the reader. The child's eyes fly across a page and ideas are taken in rapidly. Speed reading improves with variety - science and history books, mysteries and poetry. For one student, a stack of comic books in middle school morphs into novels in high school - much to the relief of that student's mother.

Phase 2. *Reads slightly below ability level.*

Reading is smooth. The reader stops at the periods and pauses at the commas. Words are pronounced correctly and, upon questioning, the meaning of the words and text are obviously understood. Independent reading is a given.

Phase 3. *Reads precisely at ability level.*

The reader is challenged with one or two unfamiliar words per page. Decoding new vocabulary with nearby clues to the meanings allows the reader to continue with only a slight interruption. Idioms and analogies are introduced. Reading is slightly difficult, but more fascinating.

A book series is appealing to this reader because familiar characters move through new adventures in recognizable places. Consider the book series Harry Potter, The Chronicles of Narnia, Ramona the Pest, Nancy

Drew, Berenstain Bears, and Sherlock Holmes. From young to old, book series capture the reader into taking many adventures through many books. Yes, a series is a serious relationship.

Phase 4. *Reads slightly above ability level.*

Although new vocabulary and unknown information is challenging, the reader wants to know more. A nearby adult supports this pursuit by answering questions and explaining vocabulary.

Phase 5. *Reads way above ability level.*

This determined reader faces several unknown words, new types of phrases, and unfamiliar ideas - per page. There is no familiar reading background. Clues to a word's meaning are seldom given as the author presumes the reader knows the vocabulary. If, because of high interest, the child genuinely wants to read the book, consider this technique. It requires an adult.

While reading out loud, the child pauses at an unfamiliar word and points to it. The adult immediately says it out loud. This makes it a sight word. A quick explanation of its meaning helps explain the sentence. A *supportive adult* is the key to a child's success when reading above ability level.

As is often true for children, once a request is satisfied, the youngster moves on. It may only take a page or a chapter for the reader to decide that the reading level is too difficult to wade through. Perhaps an easier book will satisfy the desire to learn a new topic. :)

This approach does not work for our 2nd grader who wants to read *Harry Potter*, a middle school age book. The book contains too many new words and complex concepts not yet developed. The movie may be best to satisfy her curiosity.

Summary
Reading phases include,
    1 Reads way below one's capability. Gains in speed reading.
    2 Reads with very few challenges. Enjoys many and varied topics without help.
    3 Reads on level and applies reading techniques. Independent reader.
    4 Reads above capability. Needs support.
    5 Super challenged by the difficult reading material. Extreme support is needed.

Dr. Ben Carson makes an excellent case study for the importance of reading and adults to ask questions. His story is found at the end of the Dr. Seuss lesson.
1004.E. DR. SEUSS REVISITED

> *Reading is to the mind what exercise is*
> *to the body.*
> Joseph Addison

1004.H READING GLITCHES

A 'glitch' in the reading process stops a child from reading properly Whether a physical problem with the eyes or a misunderstanding of the reading process, the child is not reading. 3 younsgters did not realize that reading is based on speech patterns.
1004.A DICTATE TO READ
1003.A IQS CAN GO UP

Chapter 4   In Conclusion
Reflect On Reading

Being able to read well is a major, lifetime achievement. It begins with a loving adult and continues in school with caring teachers. From learning to read unique letter combinations to figuring out creative interpretations, a strong reading ability is crucial to lifelong learning.

Nonreaders can learn to read quickly by being involved in writing.

- Dictating personalized booklets to an adult, 1st graders soon write and read independently.
1005. E. FIRST MONTH. FIRST GRADE AUTHORS

- Held back 2 years, 4 boys in a 2nd grade work together. Talking, writing, and reading their reading assignments as a team, their reading level jumps ahead 2 years.
1002.F FOUR BOYS SUCCEED

- The children in a small study group learn the reading process by hearing and seeing their sentences written and grammatically analyzed 'word by comma.'
1004.E DICTATE TO READ

Teaching children to read through the writing process gets my vote.

There are worse crimes than burning books.
One of them is not reading them.
Ray Bradbury

Chapter 5
Consider Writing

Train in the writing process, then begin

Topics
A. Floor Letters   B. Words From NZ   C. Frog Sentences
D. Copy to Write   E. Become an Author   F. First Time Writers
G. 5 Day Stories   H. Basic Report   I. Poetry   J. Haiku
K. Grade Papers Fast   L. Grading Rubric

Introduction
With the invention of letters, mankind develops the amazing ability to share ideas across continents and oceans and launch them into the future. Today, it's inspiring to read the thoughts of writers from an ancient civilization. Studying their writing techniques, students add them to their written work.

The writing process is taught by the teacher, discussed in study teams, and shared in group discussions. As students learn new techniques, edit each other's papers, and discuss their compositions, writing improves. Successful, independent writing is a natural consequence.

A completed assignment that receives fast feedback from the teacher impacts a student's writing favorably. With a quick and simple way for the teacher to check papers, assignments are corrected, critiqued, and returned the next day. Specific articles support a fast turnaround time.

You know I write slowly.
This is chiefly because I am never satisfied
until I have said as much as possible in a few words,
and writing briefly takes far more time than writing at length.
Carl Friedrich Gauss

Mr. Gauss is a 'deliberate' writer.

1005.A FLOOR LETTERS OF RED YARN

Five-year-old children are wiggly, so it is natural that the kindergarten teacher mentions that this alphabet lesson may be shorter than the time planned.

The class begins with an open-ended activity. Pointing to the letters posted above the white board, it's explained, "When the pointer stick touches a letter; listen for the word 'Go,' then say the letter." Pointing to the letter 'P,' 21 pairs of eyes watch. "Go!" is said loudly. "P!" they answer even more loudly. Doing 2 more for practice, the 'when to shout' process is now a given.

"Let's make a large circle on the rug. Step back to make spaces. (The children need to be far apart to reduce bumping each other.) Be as quiet as mice." We soon have a circle. My big smile and silent clapping hands tell them they are doing well.

A long piece of red yarn, is placed dramatically in the center of the circle. All eyes are on this strange event. The letter 'V' is made. Stepping outside the circle, the directions are given. "When you hear 'Go,' say the letter." They wait. "Go!" "V" they shout excitedly. A child is chosen to take the next turn. Pony tail bouncing, the five year old runs to the red yarn, makes a giant capital 'C,' then runs back to her spot on the floor and plops down. For sure, this activity has lots of action!

'Go!' 'C!' they shout. Even though they see the letter upside down, sideways, and right side up, the children recognize it. Laughter and excitement mirror their success. Every child has a turn. Every child stays focused. The lesson lasts 25 minutes.

Summarize and Celebrate!

TEACHER "What a wonderful job! Every one of you listened and watched and said the capital letters. Raise your hand, reach to the opposite shoulder. Pat yourself on the back and say, 'Great job!'" The children giggle as they pat themselves on the back, and yell "Great job!"

Their teacher takes them to their music class - a bouncing, happy, successful group.

Discussing the lesson with the teacher, we realize it engages the 3 learning styles - auditory ,visual, and kinesthetic. The visual child looks at the yarn letters and teacher. The auditory child enjoys calling out and listening to the letter names. The kinesthetic child runs to the center of the circle and bounces around when shouting the letters. Meeting everyone's learning style contributed to 100% attention.

Question. How do the kindergarteners recognize letters upside down and sideways? The answer comes from Jean Piaget's research. In the early 1900's Piaget, a Swiss psychologist, studied how young children learn. His investigations into the ways they think impacts early childhood education around the world. Teaching is more effective when it matches the young child's understanding of the environment.

Piaget investigations

1* Put 2 equal size pencils next to each other. The 4 year old agrees the pencils are the same size. Push one pencil slowly past the other so it sticks out. The child now says the pushed pencil is longer. The fact that the end also moved forward is not understood.

2* Set 2 glasses in front of a three year old - one tall and one squat. Be sure they hold the same amount of water. Fill the squat glass with water, then pour the water slowly into the tall glass. Although both glasses hold the same amount of water, the child says the taller glass holds more water.

Young children's ability to process spatially is not yet developed. For them, 'spatial direction' does not matter. Therefore, although seen from a variety of viewpoints, the capital yarn letters are recognized.

Why does a young child reverse a letter when printing a word? Knowing what the letter is, the direction it faces has no meaning. When the visual-spatial ability develops, the letter is printed in the right direction.

Summary
The lesson meets the steps of *Teaching! It's All In the Process.*
1. The open ended board activity focuses the students on the procedure.
2. The presentation is the names of the letters.
3. For collaboration, the students make letters and shouted letter names.
4. To summarize the activity is reviewed. Celebration is praise and a pat on the back.

A specific teaching process combined with learning styles, produces a powerhouse, child-centered activity. Everyone learns and has a wonderful time!
Play is the work of childhood.
Jean Piaget

1005.B WORDS FROM NEW ZEALAND
Sylvia Ashton-Warner of New Zealand publishes her book *Teacher* in 1963. As the British method for teaching reading does not work for the indigenous Maori children, she develops a unique and successful methodology. Reading her book. I am intrigued by her 'how to teach reading' method.

Every day, Miss Warner asks each child for a word that he wants to be able to read. Printing it on a large card, the child reads it aloud, and places it in a personally decorated box. This 'Treasure Chest' is taken home at night and brought back the next day. At home, both the child and parents practice the words.

For the first time, a teacher responds to the specific educational needs of the students and parents. Honoring her research and success, countries around the world rewrite early childhood curriculum to meet the young child's unique way of learning. The basis is child-centered activities.

Summary
It's with much gratitude that Sylvia's name and book is mentioned. Her focus on the child's needs impacts my teaching. Over the years, it becomes clear that adjusting the teaching process to create student success is easier than adjusting the students.

Sylvia's book is available on amazon.com. Her 'word technique' is on page 127. She emphasizes that the words the children choose have an emotional value. A whole set of feelings and stories are embedded with the word. This makes it easy to transform the word into a short story.
1004.C LEARN TO READ BY WRITING

> *To improve is to change, to be perfect is to change often.*
> Winston Churchill

1005.C FROG SENTENCES: 2 TO 22 WORDS.
Bobby stares at the floor dejectedly as his mom explains the problem. "His teacher says he writes 3 words and stops." Bobby looks up sadly. "I can't think of anything."

The problem to be solved is, "How do you teach a child to have more ideas?"

A new idea pops. (An advantage of one on one tutoring is new inspiration can be tried on the spur of the moment.) Can a short sentence be expanded by using grammar questions? Would Bobby understand that specific questions lead to more ideas and more writing?

On a piece of paper, two words are printed at the top. His answer to each grammar question will form longer sentences. As the sentences are written for him, his job is to think.

Frogs hop.

TEACHER "What does this sentence say?"
BOBBY "Frogs hop."
TEACHER "Excellent."

Description questions are asked.
TEACHER "What color describes the frog?" (adjective)
BOBBY "Green."
The longer sentence is written below the first one.

Frogs hop.
Green frogs hop.

Again, he reads the sentence. We continue.
TEACHER "What size describes the frog?"
BOBBY "Big."

Frogs hop.
Green frogs hop.
Big, green frogs hop.

His eyes light up. His sentence is growing. He reads it aloud.
Next, the action is described. (adverb)
TEACHER **"How do frogs hop?"**
BOBBY "High."

Frogs hop.
Green frogs hop.
Big, green frogs hop.
Big, green frogs hop high.

Bobby is delighted! His eyes are as wide-eyed as a frog's! He laughs as more words are added.

How are the frogs feeling? (happy.)
Where do they hop? (into the air.)
How do they hop? (wildly.)
Where are the frogs? (in the pond.)

Happy, big green frogs hop high.
Happy, big green frogs hop high **into the air.**
Happy, big green frogs hop **wildly** and high into the air.
In the pond, happy, big green frogs hop wildly and high into the air.

TEACHER "Why do the frogs hop?"
BOBBY "Because they see an owl."
In the pond, happy, big green frogs hop wildly and high into the air **because they see an owl.**

The word 'owl' means one more question is asked.
TEACHER "Where is the owl?"
BOBBY "In a tree."
His sentence is complete.

In the pond happy, big green frogs hop wildly and high into the air because they see an owl **in the tree**.

Bobby counts his words. - 22! When his mom returns, her son excitedly reads his sentence aloud and announces, "It has 22 words!" He explains how he added details about the frogs by answering questions. This is one happy child. Mom and I are happy, too.

A class lesson
To introduce the grammar question and answer method in the classroom, a sample is explained. Then, given 2 words, student teams ask questions

and write their answers. Laughter, a 'research-proven sign of 'creativity popping and intelligence morphing,' fills the room. Both students sign their names on the paper. Spelling counts. The next day, they share their sentences. Students now understand how to enrich sentence writing.

To summarize the longest sentence, an illustration is drawn with the sentence printed at the bottom. To celebrate their work, the children hang them in the hallway and watch students stop and read them.

For these examples, students change 'it' to a noun and have individualized sentence starters. It barks. It shines. It zooms. It drizzles. It falls. It purrs. It writes.

Summary
A key to students' writing success is lots of vocabulary words for the assignment. With grammar questions, Bobby's vocabulary and sentence expanded. Older students challenge themselves to identify unique and distinct words with a thesaurus.

Note. A high IQ and complex vocabulary are related.

Story
One year, it is clear that the 5th graders no longer recall the grammar rules taught in the earlier grades. The 5th grade curriculum does not include a grammar review.

Based on their previous grammar textbooks, specific lessons are taught twice a week for 45 minutes each, The students are surprised to discover how many grammar rules they have forgotten. Alert to the rules, their writing improves.
1002.D STUDENTS AS EDITORS

Grammar, which knows how to control even kings.
Moliere

1005.D Copy To Learn To Write

Animals and people learn life skills by mimicking. The gosling swims behind its mother and mimics her techniques in finding food. The human baby practices 'mama' to get her attention. For hours, a future basketball star dribbles and tosses the ball with her dad. At school, assignments are sent home for skill practice. To mimic and gain positive results requires a suitable example.

Introduce story writing
A short story dictated by the class is written on the board by the teacher. As each sentence is written, 'pondering' questions are asked out loud. Hearing the teacher's thoughts, provides new ideas to consider. For instance, "What will happen if a storm comes? Will the lost puppy wander into a mall?" "What if a $50 bill is found?"

Because the teacher is writing, the students do not worry about spelling and proper grammar. While copying the story, the students are encouraged to add new details to individualize and enrich their work. Sharing the stories with their study partner leads to more ideas.
1005.F Third Graders. First Time Writers.

Summary
As the teacher demonstrates a variety of writing techniques, students learn them as they copy the sentences. Encouraged to change sentences and add details, student confidence improves. Independent writing begins with copying.

> *I know I was writing stories when I was five.*
> *I don't know what I did before that.*
> *Just loafed I suppose.*
> P.G. Wodehouse

1005.E First Month. First Grade Authors.

It's the 2nd day of the school year. A first grade teacher asks me to observe her class at the start of the day. It is a surprise to see each student sitting next to an adult. The adult volunteer is recording the child's book dictation. The teacher is conducting a reading group.

Background
During Open House, when parents meet teachers, this teacher enlists parents to help her class write books during the first few weeks of school. Parents sign up for a day and time. A direction sheet for 'How to help a child write a book' is provided. School personnel sign up to help during their break times. The night before the adult's scheduled day, the teacher calls to be sure the dictation process is clear. These volunteers are the mainstay of the students' amazing book accomplishments.

The booklets are a couple of pages with lines at the bottom folded and stapled. One sentence is written on each page. Watching their book being written, the students learn how words look (spelling) and how they become sentences (grammar). A book title is written on the front cover with the author's name written underneath. Illustrations are drawn by the students. This unique combination of adults and students creates a solid foundation for understanding the writing-reading process.

In 2 weeks, the box of 'alphabetized-by-last-name' booklets is full! The authors proudly read their books aloud to everyone - a friend, a small group, or to the whole class. Hearing books read aloud, broadens the children's ideas. For instance, when a person's name is used, other children start to use names in their stories. Theme charts, including the basic vocabulary, such as Pet Words or Fall Words are posted in the room.

The children soon become independent writers. In the reading groups, the teacher uses the curriculum stories to emphasize interpretations and implications.

Summary
The devotion of these adults creates a nurturing environment for this authentic learning activity. At the end of the 1ˢᵗ semester, the entire class is on grade level (or beyond) in reading and writing skills. Every child learns, shares, helps others, and becomes an independent author and reader. It's truly an authentic one room school house.

Story
This teacher fine-tuned her process over the years, and it worked perfectly for her. Years later, a version is tried in my 1ˢᵗ grade. Students write a story which I type during class time. It is thought that illustrating their story would keep the children busy while stories are typed. That did not happen. Stories are typed at home. Adult volunteers are the key as they keep everyone busy until they are independent writers.

> *A reading man or woman is a ready man and woman,*
> *but a writing man and woman is exact.*
> Marcus Garvey

1005.F THIRD GRADERS. FIRST TIME WRITERS.
The two 3ʳᵈ grade classes have never written a story - not even a sentence. Hoping the children will write for a different teacher, their teachers invite me to teach a writing lesson.

Day 1
Two boys sit in the front row chuckling. They are friends and excited to work together. Others sit quietly with their writing partners, attentive and perhaps wondering what this teacher is going to teach. By request, the teachers have paired the class by ability level. Independent teams are seated in the back of the room while deliberate workers are in the front. After introducing myself, we begin.

TEACHER "What are you learning in science?" Answers fly as they tell facts about astronomy.

TEACHER "I understand that comets haven't been taught, right?" They nod.
TEACHER "Great. I'll read about comets from these library books, then you tell me what details you remember."

Note. Secondary research is modeled by reading the title, author, and page numbers.

At the end of 10 minutes, the lesson shifts its focus to the students.
TEACHER "Tell your partner the comet facts you remember. Take turns." The room fills with happy, babbling voices. No one is sitting quietly except the 2 teachers in the back of the room who are probably wondering, "Will these children write?"

The word 'comet' is written on the board.
TEACHER "Let's stop now and share what you know. Your facts will be written around the word comet." Everyone's hands waves. (For me, it's a delightful moment when every child knows they know and wants everyone else to know they know.) The 2 boys are called on first to ensure their facts aren't used by someone else. Writing their facts with a flourish and praise - Good job! - the boys beam. Hands wave. Facts fly. The board is soon covered with facts about comets.

Now comes the challenging part of the lesson. Not one child in this 3rd grade has ever written a sentence much less a story or report - not in Kindergarten, 1st, 2nd and, until now, not in 3rd grade. The parents, teachers, principal, and counselor are baffled. The advantage of this lesson is the 3rd graders don't know that I know. The focus on the facts now shifts to writing.

TEACHER "Look at all the comet words. With your partner, use them to write 2 sentences about comets. Each sentence must have at least 10 words." Without a pause, everyone starts writing. A student in the back of the room calls out, "Can the sentence be longer?"

TEACHER "Of course, see if you can get to 22 words."
"Wow!" exclaims the 2 boys in front. "We'll do that, too!"

Considered 'poor' learners, it is hoped that these 2 boys would at least pay attention. Instead, pencils racing, they go to work. Hearing children count their words, I realize that competition with the number 22 is pushing their effort. Who would have guessed?

A few minutes later, the 1 hour writing session ends and their papers are collected. It's time for praise.
TEACHER Pointing to the board. "Look at all the facts you remembered." Waving the papers. "Your sentences look long. We'll share them tomorrow." No one had any idea they were going to write a paragraph the next day.

Day 2
The children stand up in pairs and share their sentences. Everyone talks, everyone listens. Confidence grows. Failure is not an option. In fact, with all the ideas read aloud, it is no longer possible.

Next is the parts of a paragraph. A title is described as 'short, but of high interest.' A student contributes a sample which is written on the board. Opening and closing sentences are explained. "An opening sentence captures the reader's attention. The closing sentence makes it clear the information is finished." Simple samples are written on the board.

The writing partners are asked to discuss other titles and sentences. The room is abuzz. No pressure. A partner makes it safe. The words on the board make it safe. Success is guaranteed!

TEACHER "Each of you take a new piece of paper and put your name and date at the top right. Write a title and an opening sentence. Then copy your 'yesterday sentences.' At the end, write the closing sentence. Remember, you can copy this title and sentences or write your own. "

The class, including the 2 boys, starts to write. A student asks, "Can we add new sentences?" The answer is, "Of course." This question proves the students are individualizing their assignment to the level that challenges them.

The reports are complete. The teachers promise the class to let them draw pictures. They'll be posted in the hall with their reports. Leaving the comet books on a counter, the children are encouraged to find new facts to share.

Two weeks later
Walking past the classroom, the 2 teachers are posting new writing assignments and illustrations. We smile at each other. The 3rd graders are now writers - including our 2 boys.

Background
The day before the 2 lessons, I visit a class. As the children enter the room, they are highly active and not paying attention to their teacher's directions. This scattered behavior is reversed the next day by asking the students to stop at the door. As they gather there, directions are given. Come in quietly, sit with hands folded, and look directly at the teacher.

"This," said firmly with a smile, "will tell me that you are ready for the lesson." Kindness and clearly stated directions are important to their transformation. They readily follow the new procedure.

Summary
The students' high interest in comets, the variety of books read, and an interactive approach keeps the class 100% involved. With vocabulary on the board and partners sitting next to them, their fear of writing evaporates. The challenge of a 22 word sentence is a surprise bonus.

These 2 teachers had hesitated to invite another teacher into the room. With years of the students' resistance to writing, it is a concern that the children will act up. On the 2ⁿᵈ day, the principal, vice principal, and counselor join us. The new 3ʳᵈ grade authors make everyone's day.

Employ your time in improving yourself by other men's writings,
so that you shall gain easily what others have labored hard for.
Socrates

1005.G 5 Days to Fabulous Stories

Note. The writing process used in the previous 3ʳᵈ grade now expands into a weeklong lesson.

Story
A new 1ˢᵗ grade teacher asks her students to write a new story every day. The children aren't coping well. In fact, they stop trying.

Told one of her students has a tutor, she calls for help. A 5 day writing process is suggested. It's explained, "Beginning writers need time to absorb each step of the writing process. By spreading the steps over 5 days, the children go home at night and think about what they learned. Over time, they'll write stories faster."

Day 1 Introduce the topic
Car Racing
Ask, "What do you know about cars? About car racing?" Read excerpts and show pictures from a variety of books and magazines. Show a video. "What do you think is hard or easy to do in car racing?"

Day 2 Identify vocabulary
"What facts do you remember about car racing?" "What words will help you write about car racing?" Print the words where they will be available for the week. To expand ideas, ask questions about the parts of the car; race track words, and descriptive words including colors and sounds.

Day 3 Write sentences
TEACHER "What sentences can you make with these words?"
Teams discuss, then share their sentences aloud. Sentences are written on the board.
STUDENTS "Cars get gas. One car wins. The noise is loud. The gun goes off. The winner gets the checkered flag. A tire is changed."

Day 4 Identify a title and opening and closing sentences
Children reread the vocabulary and sentences. Introduce the 3 parts of a report. Write them vertically leaving spaces for their story sentences.

Race Day
The cars line up.
_____
_____
_____
The winners get the flag.

TEACHER "A key idea tells what the story is about. It's called the title. Name some titles."
STUDENTS "The Car Race" "Race Day"
TEACHER "An opening sentence is a fact that tells that the story is beginning. Tell a sentence begins the story."
STUDENTS "The cars get ready." "Race day has arrived. "
TEACHER "A closing sentence tells us the race is over. Tell a closing sentence."
STUDENTS "The race is over." "The green car got the flag."

Day 5 Time to write stories
First, the children review the board sentences and vocabulary.

TEACHER "Let's use our ideas to write our story. You tell me what to write, and I'll put it on the board."
When it's done, the children copy the story and add details, or write their own. To copy more easily, some children are seated near the board.

As they finish writing, encourage them to read their stories to each other. With race car books and magazines on the interest table, students read and share new facts and pictures. When the stories are done, it's time for illustrations.

Note. If a child brings their own model car, decide when to share it and where to keep it safe.

Summary

Reading information aloud, reduces student stress, enriches their vocabulary, and improves IQs. Working in study teams develops understanding and builds confidence. Related books and magazines on the interest table lead to more ideas to share. As writing has several components to consider, a 5 day process makes it clear and easy.

Easy reading is extremely hard writing.
Nathanial Hawthorne

1005.H BASIC REPORT - DINOSAURS

Background
The district's 'low ability' 2nd graders are divided into 2 classrooms in the same school. A dinosaur unit is taught in the science class. The 2nd grade teachers ask for a simple report method to use for future writing. Simple graphics organize the process.

An open-ended question starts the lesson. "What do you know about dinosaurs?" Answers are recorded at the top of the board.

Dinosaurs

| big | scary | long | ate plants | ate animals | long ago | long teeth |
| long tail | laid eggs | had nests | died long ago | some fly | bones found |

Note. To improve word recognition, words are pointed to and the students read them aloud. It's done more than once to build sight vocabulary.

Four boxes with simple labels are drawn on the board.

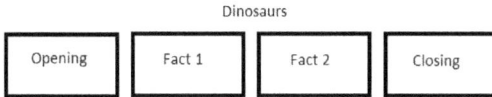

Dinosaurs

Opening	Fact 1	Fact 2	Closing

TEACHER "Let's organize your words by writing them under the boxes." The students words are written on the board.

Dialogue.
Box 1: "To capture the reader's attention, we need 'opening' facts.' Which facts are the most interesting?"
Box 2: "What words tell what dinosaurs eat?"
Box 3: "What words are about dinosaur babies?
Box 4: "To end our report, which facts mean the dinosaur report is finished?

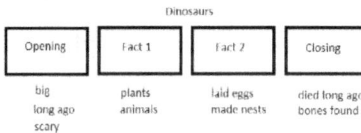

Dinosaurs

Opening	Fact 1	Fact 2	Closing
big long ago scary	plants animals	laid eggs made nests	died long ago bones found

Next, the study teams think of a sentence to match each box. As the class shares their sentences, they are written under each box.

Dialogue
*Box 1 "With your team partner, think of a sentence to begin the report. One will be written on the board."
 'Long ago lives scary, big dinosaurs.' or 'Big, scary dinosaurs live long ago.'
*Box 2 "Using your facts, think of a sentence that tells about dinosaurs and plants?"
'The dinosaurs eat plants and animals.' or 'Dinosaur food is plants and animals.'

*Box 3 "Think of a sentence about the babies."
'Mama dinosaurs make nests. They lay eggs.' Or 'After making nests, Mama dinosaurs lay eggs inside.'
*Box 4 "Think of a sentence to tell that the dinosaurs are gone."
'Dinosaurs died long ago. All that's left are bones.' or ' After the dinosaurs die, only their bones are left.'

Writing the report.
TEACHER
 "Put your name and date at the top of your paper. Write the title in the middle at the top. Choose and write 1 or 2 sentences from under each box."
Note. These steps do not happen fast. This writing process is a 2 day activity.

It's time to write. Three children sit up front to copy the sentences. For one child, the teacher writes the first word of a sentence, then the child copies the rest.

The classroom teachers provide extra time to complete their reports. Pictures are drawn and, with the reports, are posted in the room.

Dropping by to visit a week later, a spaghetti making activity in the adjoining kitchen is in full swing with lots of mom

volunteers. The reports come next. This real life experience will provide ideas to keep the 2nd graders writing.

Summary
Although these 2nd grade classes are considered low functioning, the short and simple steps are easily followed and learned. The teachers use this method for the rest of the year. According to them, the children show 'more than expected' progress on their national tests - almost and

sometimes - reaching grade level test scores. Congratulations to the children and their teachers.

All things are difficult before they are [made] easy.
Thomas Fuller

1005.I PHOTOS TO POETRY

A 1st grade teacher asks to have poetry introduced to her students. With Spring in the air, it's decided that photos of the school neighborhood will be made into slides.

"What words describe Spring?" Writing their words on chart paper with a small drawing next to it helps the children's recall. Showing the slides, student attention is an excited 100%! They recognize their neighborhood New words are added to the chart.

Examples
icicles sky violet leaves leaf cold muddy warm puddles flowers snow clouds fluffy

With chart words and study teams, thinking of Spring sentences is a success. Their sentences are written on the board.
Examples
The icicle is dripping. The snow is muddy. There are puddles. Flowers are coming up. The sky is blue.

The next day, we begin with a handout of 3 poems *not based on* their words. The study teams read them aloud to each other.

Spring
Petals open.
Purple and violet
Flowers.

Sky
Wind blows.
Blue and white
Clouds.

Icicles
Water drips.
Gray and brown
Puddles.

TEACHER "Let's figure out how the poems are alike? Look at the first word in each poem. (A star next to the words makes it easy to focus on them). What makes them the same?
STUDENTS "It tells one idea." "It's in the slides."
TEACHER "Let's look at the last word. How does it fit with the first one?" Write the 2 words next to each other. Spring-Flower Sky-Clouds Icicles-Puddles
STUDENTS "The ideas connect."

TEACHER "What does the 2nd line do?" (Action.)
Circle the action words. Petals *open.* Wind *blows.* Water *drips.*
STUDENTS "It tells something is happening."

TEACHER "Let's look at the words in line 3. How are they alike?"
STUDENTS "Color words."

TEACHER "Our poems have four parts - a title, action, 2 colors, a word that connects to the title. Let's use the pattern for a class poem."
The teacher writes it on the board.
   - What's a starting word? (Clouds)
   - What action do clouds have? (Float high)
   - Which color words fit clouds? (Yellow and pink)
   - What word connects back to the first word? (Sunset)

Note. This author and editor agree. These are so much fun to do, we could write a book.

As the class begins writing their poems, options for completing the assignment contribute to success. Options include individual writing, 2 children write together, the board poem or one on the handout is copied, writers write more than one poem.

The classroom teacher provides time for drawing. They celebrate their work by reading their poems to the class and hanging them in the hallway.
1003.C INDIVIDUALIZE TO SURPASS SAMENESS

Summary
Analyzing the poems identifies a simple pattern that guarantees success for every child. Samples and a class poem reduce stress and clarifies expectations. This is a 2 day lesson.

With many options to write a poem, children choose one that reflects their ability. It is a wonderful way to learn about Spring.

It is clear to everyone who walks past the 1st grade classroom and sees their poems and illustrations, Spring is here. The poets are excited to see other students stop to read their poems.

> *Poetry is when an emotion has found its thought*
> *and the thought has found words.*
> Robert Frost

1005.J SEASONS AND HAIKU
Note. This activity enriches a science leaf lesson found in lesson 1007.A.

To explain haiku, examples are shared. First, the students identify the syllables. Note. Syllables are the parts of a word heard when the word is spoken aloud.

To show the syllables in the poems, the students put dots above them. The syllable pattern is discussed.

The haiku pattern.
- Line 1: 5 syllables
- Line 2: 7 syllables
- Line 3: 5 syllables.

Other rules are,
- No rhyming.
- Ideas are based on clues to seasons. (Fall: leaves falling, geese flying South; cooler days)
- 'Every day feelings' are emphasized.

Using the Haiku samples, study teams write their own by copying a sample with changes or by writing an original poem.

Winter Comes

Summer light softens. 2-1-2 = 5
Overhead, gray geese fly South. 3-1-1-1-1 = 7
Leaves float with delight.   1-1-1-2 = 5

Spring Morning

Gentle breezes drift past. 2-1-1-1 = 5
Dewdrops form on spider webs. 2-1-1-2-1 = 7
The heart sparkles joy. 1-1-2-1 = 5

Thunder Rolls

Lightning flashes white. 2-2-1 = 5
Black clouds loudly roar thunder 1-1-2-1-2= 7
Knees quake, fear happens. 1-1-1-2 = 5

Note. These young poets gave a poetry recital during a school wide activity.

Summary
Poetry uses unique patterns. For the students, connecting ideas in a poem is a different approach to expressing thoughts and feelings.

Poetry book
For 3 weeks the 5th graders write several types of poetry. Listing the rules for each poem, then writing a sample and drawing an illustration, their final pages form a booklet of original poems. To preserve the integrity of their book, comments and grades are written on a separate piece of paper which is paperclipped to the booklet

It's a suggestion that they save it (in a drawer where soft clothing is kept.) in case a middle school teacher assigns the same poetry project. One teacher does. A youngster returns to share that he has the same grade.

*Writing a book of poetry is like dropping a rose petal
down the Grand Canyon and waiting for the echo.*
Don Marquis

*I hope this quote doesn't hold true for writing a book about teaching.
Laughter!*

1005.K GRADE WRITING ASSIGNMENTS, FAST!

It's true. With lots of practice, students become better writers. However, it takes time to grade stories and essays. First, reduce corrections and improve student techniques.

- Review grammar rules regularly, so student mistakes are fewer.
- Brainstorm and post vocabulary to reduce spelling mistakes.
- Teach students how to edit each other's papers.
- Apply this grading process. The micro-steps require a learning curve, but when the process becomes familiar, grading is a breeze.
- Post the assignment criteria so they are clear, and everyone finds them easy to follow.
- Encourage teamwork.

Clear, quick criteria
- Describe the setting sun with color words. What color words do we know? What does the sun and clouds do when the sun is setting?
- Tell what a plant experiences in the rain and sun. Remember the parts of the plant and its roots beneath the sod.
- Write an adventure story about a lost pet finding its way home. Where is the pet? What situations are happening around it?
- The electricity is out. What happens next? Think of each room. What happens when it's time to eat?

Time to grade
With your stack of wonderfully written stories based on criteria and edited by class editors, it's time to grade.

Procedure
- Place a chair so there's a large space in front of it.
- Imagine the top half of a clock is in front of you. Nine is to the left and three is to the right. This diagram describes the grades.

Grade Fast!

B
Well done.

A
Excellent.

12

11

9

C
Got it.

1

3

D
Needs help.

Read and react quickly to each paper. Speed is of the essence.
- Review the criteria ,
- Read a paper and toss it onto the number that describes it.
- Skim through each stack of papers to be sure the stack is 'on the same page' with a similar level of accomplishment.
- Move a page to a different stack as needed.

Grading guidelines
 9 o'clock 'A.' Well done with a creative application of criteria.
 11 o'clock 'B' The criteria are clearly applied.
 1 o'clock 'C.' Papers are decent, but need organization or details.
 3 o'clock 'D' These papers will benefit from a team or a class review as described in 1002.D STUDENTS AS EDITORS.

If a + and – are wanted, rearrange the papers in each stack so the better written ones are on top, and the 'not as well written' ones are on the bottom. Put a + on the better ones, and – on the 'not as well written.'

As children tend to toss papers after they are done, - for them assignments are about the journey not the destination - collect and save them. If a new assignment needs too much time to complete, hand out a previous one. Ask the children to share a favorite part with the class. After hearing new ideas, the class is ready to rewrite their essay or story.

Summary

When students review their large collection of assignments, it encourages
 their confidence in writing. Whether they copy the class example,
change out a few words, work as a team, or write individually, all
assignments are completed. This is good for the child's self- image.

Note. When using them at parent conferences, be sure to ask for them
back for student rewriting. Or, make the parent a copy.

Children have to be educated, but they also have
to be left to educate themselves.
Ernest Dimnet

1005.L GRADE WITH A RUBRIC

Analyzing assignments with a rubric takes more time. It's suggested that
this method is used only when a detailed analysis of the students' work is
the goal.

Begin
To introduce the parts of writing, use a theme to teach one aspect at a
time: Title. Opening sentence. Interesting details. Closing sentence. An
exciting statement. A question. Etc.

Specific criteria are precisely explained. The opening sentence can
require up to 3 aspects: time, place, and a hint of the event to come.

Basic opening. One day the campers go fishing.
More precise opening. As the sun rises over the mountain, the campers
hear the sound of fish jumping.

These points rank each criteria.
5 Well done! 4 Rather good.   3 Poorly done.   2 Not done.
Please, no ones or zeroes. It drops the average too much.

Assignment_____ Date_____

Student	Opening	Closing	Good Details	Proper Grammar	Vocabular Words	Punctuation	Spelling	Total Points
Points-	5	5	5	5	5	5	5	35
101								
102								
103								
104								

This rubric lists the total scores. Child 101, might have an Opening score of '5', Closing a 4', Good Details a '4,' Proper grammar a '5', etc. Total the student's points. See chart for grades. Although a major undertaking, a rubric gives a detailed analysis of the children's writing.

Grades based on 55 points									
55	100%	A+	31	89%	B+	27	77%	C+	24	69%	D+
54	97%	A+	50	86%	B	26	74%	C	25	66%	D
53	94%	A	29	83%	B	25	71%	C	22	65%	D
52	91%	A	28	80%	B				21	60%	D

Any lower grades stay at 50% and D.
Have the class edit these papers without the child's name.
To make them anonymous, type them up.

Summary
For the teacher, a rubric scoring procedure requires more time and thought. However, its detailed analysis indicates how the class and individuals are progressing. When it is time to decide what the children need to learn most about writing, here is a way to find out.
1002.D STUDENTS AS EDITORS

Civilization began the first time an angry person
cast a word instead of a rock.
Sigmund Freud

CHAPTER 5 IN CONCLUSION
CONSIDER WRITING

To make the role of writing components thought-provoking, connect the different aspects to other subjects. For instance

Replace the 'opening sentence' in a science paragraph. Instead of 'Bacteria eat oil,' create 'New bacteria eat the spilled oil. Fish starve.'

Replace the closing sentence in the 2nd grade race car story about the yellow car cheating with "The yellow car grabs the trophy, and speeds away"

Reverse the events of history. The introductory sentence of a paragraph about England's taxes on the colonists, might change to, "King George III cancels taxes. Colonists cancel rebellion."

Connect facts to build a 22 word sentence. 'Abe built' becomes, "In 1829, Abe Lincoln, who became the 16th U.S. President, built a log cabin in the woods of Indiana when he was 20 years old. (Counting numbers and abbreviations, 25 words)

Identify writing components in other subjects, then change them. Their role and importance becomes clearer for the students.

The difference between the almost right word
and the right word is really a large matter –
'tis the difference between a lightning-bug and the lightning.
Mark Twain

Chapter 6
Discover Math

Start with hands-on, compute with reason

Topics
A 10 Facts   B. Long Addition   C. Multiplication Tactics
D. Finger Multiplication   E. Math Formulas   F. Coins   G. Time
H. Make Fractions   I. Compare Fractions
J. Measure Tree Height

Introduction

Math's strange behaviors of different types of numbers reveals complex math procedures. For instance, multiplying fractions results in a smaller number while dividing them produces a larger one. Rules for basic computations change radically. A math unit of decimals, percents, fractions, time, measurement and percents includes its own rules for addition and subtraction, division, and multiplication.

To prepare students for a new math unit means teaching a specialized language. Like entering a new country, communication in the new language must be specifically taught and defined with illustrations and examples. A *quarter to 2* is not the same as 4 *quarters* in a dollar or a *quarter of* a pizza. The 'language of fractions' or the 'language of time' or the 'language of money' reveals similar words with new meanings. Passports, anyone?

> *Mathematics is the art of giving the same*
> *name to different things.*
> Henri Poincare

1006.A ADDITION 10 FACTS

Young children enjoy the brilliant colors of bingo chips. After a few moments of play, they are ready to discover 2-digit addition facts with sums of 10. The hands on, visual, and auditory learners are totally engaged. (KVA)

Each math team is given a baggie of 20 plastic bingo chips, paper, and pencils. Putting the group's names inside each baggie makes having the bingo chips a big deal. The children count the chips before and after each lesson. None are lost.

Introduce a number sentence that equals 10 on a smart board or overhead.
Note. The dialogue replaces long paragraphs. :)

TEACHER "Today, we're going to use bingo chips to discover addition number sentences that equal 10." (Spread out 10 chips. Write = 10. Touch each one as the students count them aloud.)
"Let's count the chips. 1, 2....10."
 Next, slowly separate them into 2 groups, perhaps 7 and 3.

TEACHER "How many chips are in each small group?" Point to each chip as the children count them aloud.
STUDENTS "1,2,3,4,5,6,7...seven, and 1.2.3...three."

TEACHER Slowly and dramatically push the chips *one by one* from the small group into the large one. "Let's count how many 7 chips and 3 chips make."
STUDENTS "1,2,3,4,5,6,7,8,9,10...ten!"
The children now have a procedure for finding the 10 math sentences.'

TEACHER "What number sentence explains how the 2 groups were pushed together? Whisper your answer to your study partner."
STUDENTS "3 + 7 = 10 or 7 + 3 = 10"
Write the 2 number sentences on the board.
TEACHER "You said 2 number sentences. How can that be?"

STUDENTS "Because it doesn't matter. …Because the rule is 'Adding either way is okay.' …We used the same numbers."

TEACHER "Yes. A rule in math addition is 'the order of adding numbers can be different.'" Write the rule on the board.
Move the chips around to show 7+3, and then move them back to show 3+7. (This helps the children who need to see the idea and see the movement.)

TEACHER "With your math team partner, use the chips to figure out more number sentences. Write them both ways." As the children work, encourage discussion and 'figuring things out.' Those who are done early can rewrite the sentences in an organized pattern starting with 1+9 = 10 through 9+1 = 10.
Note. Some children may realize 0+10 and 10+0 are number sentences for 10.
1001.E COLLABORATION

Summarize
TEACHER "Let's have a math team volunteer to write a number sentence on the board. If you have the same number sentence on your paper, put a red star." Children take turns until all sentences are recorded.

$$\text{Addition Ten Facts}$$

$1 + 9 = 10$	$6 + 4 = 10$
$2 + 8 = 10$	$7 + 3 = 10$
$3 + 7 = 10$	$8 + 2 = 10$
$4 + 6 = 10$	$9 + 1 = 10$
$5 + 5 = 10$	

TEACHER "Your number sentences are called *addition facts*. How many do you have?" (9) (Unless 0's are used, then there are 11.)

Enrich addition facts

Writing addition facts with cat faces improves long term memory. KVA:
The 'process' of drawing is recalled by children who like movement.
Talking ideas over with a team member meets the auditory child's needs.
The visual child remembers seeing cat facts.
1011.H HOW LEARNING HAPPENS - AVK

Triangles or circles can form cat faces. Use a previous number sentence
that equals 10 with the word 'cats.'
8 *cats* + 2 *cats* = 10 *cats*
Draw the picture.

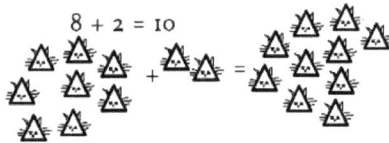

Assignment. The children choose and write a number sentence with cats
or another simply drawn figure.
1003.C INDIVIDUALIZE TO SURPASS SAMENESS

Summary
Activities and discussion keep the students 100% involved. Using bingo
chips to explain and drawing pictures leads to long term recall.
Memorizing the addition facts, the students can move to the next stages
of addition.
Note. Let children count with their fingers. These are usually the
kinesthetic children who need movement.

*Mathematical discoveries, like springtime violets in the woods, they have
their season which no human can hasten or retard.*
Carl Friedrich Gauss

1006.B A 'LONG' ADDITION PROBLEM
The 2nd graders are writing and adding number sentences with sums of 9

or less such as $3 + 2 = 5$ and $7 + 1 = 8$. As the practice work becomes labor intensive, it's clear a fresh approach is needed.

TEACHER "You are doing a great job adding 2 numbers. Do you know you can now add really long numbers?"
STUDENTS "No way!"
TEACHER "Let me show you how. Turn over your practice paper. Carefully copy this line of digits. As you write each digit, leave a small space so the next digit doesn't bump into the one before.
Note. Make sure the 2 digits add up to 9 or less.

$$7\ 2\ 1\ 8\ 3\ 6\ 0\ 2\ 4\ 5$$

TEACHER "Compare your digits with your math partner to be sure you both have all ten digits in the correct order."
TEACHER "Underneath each digit, we are going to write another digit. Under the 5 write a 3; under the 4, write a 1." Along we go.

$$7\ 2\ 1\ 8\ 3\ 6\ 0\ 2\ 4\ 5$$
$$2\ 4\ 6\ 1\ 3\ 2\ 9\ 5\ 1\ 3$$

TEACHER "Because this is an addition problem, we draw a line under the bottom row of numbers."
TEACHER "Because we're adding, put a plus sign on the left."

$$\begin{array}{r} 7\ 2\ 1\ 8\ 3\ 6\ 0\ 2\ 4\ 5 \\ +\ 2\ 4\ 6\ 1\ 3\ 2\ 9\ 5\ 1\ 3 \\ \hline \end{array}$$

TEACHER "Let's do this! Look at each top number and add it to the number under it. The sum goes underneath the line." (Point to the numbers as you explain.)

TEACHER "When adding long numbers, we always start on the right side which is the 5 and the 3. What does $5 + 3$ equal?"
STUDENTS "8."
The teacher prints an 8 under the 3. The children copy.

TEACHER "Who can tell us the next 2 numbers to add?"
All hands go up.
TEACHER "Tell your neighbor first." The children whisper excitedly.
TEACHER "Let's say the 2 numbers together."
STUDENTS "4 plus 1."
TEACHER "What's the answer?
STUDENTS "5!"
TEACHER "Let's write it down." We do.

The children are now on their own. Eagerly, they add the rest of the numbers. When everyone is done, they compare their answers with their math partner.

$$\begin{array}{r} 7\ 2\ 1\ 8\ 3\ 6\ 0\ 2\ 4\ 5 \\ +\ 2\ 4\ 6\ 1\ 3\ 2\ 9\ 5\ 1\ 3 \\ \hline 9\ 6\ 7\ 9\ 6\ 8\ 9\ 7\ 5\ 8 \end{array}$$

TEACHER "You are all amazing! For our next activity, let's start a board list of addition facts that add up to nine or less." The children contribute, the teacher writes.

TEACHER "With your math partner, write a long number problem using the number facts on the board that *add up only to 9*. Then you'll trade with another math team who checks your problem."

$$\begin{array}{r} 3\ 4\ 2\ 7\ 1\ 8\ 9\ 5\ 6\ 4\ 7 \\ +\ 6\ 5\ 7\ 2\ 8\ 1\ 0\ 4\ 3\ 5\ 2 \\ \hline 9\ 9\ 9\ 9\ 9\ 9\ 9\ 9\ 9\ 9\ 9 \end{array}$$

As another challenge, ask the children to create a pattern in which sums are 2 alternating numbers. For instance,

$$\begin{array}{r} 4\ 8\ 2\ 6\ 3\ 9\ 1\ 4\ 3\ 8\ 2\ 4\ 5\ 7 \\ +1\ 1\ 3\ 3\ 2\ 0\ 4\ 5\ 2\ 1\ 3\ 5\ 0\ 2 \\ \hline 5\ 9\ 5\ 9\ 5\ 9\ 5\ 9\ 5\ 9\ 5\ 9\ 5\ 9 \end{array}$$

Summary
The children learn addition facts by adding long numbers. As every child is operating at their own level of ability and in a team, everyone succeeds. Sharing their patterns with other students leads to progress and growth in higher levels of thinking. With repetition and analysis, memorization happens.

> *Happiness lies in the joy of the achievement*
> *and the thrill of the creative effort.*
> Franklin D. Roosevelt

1006.C MULTIPLICATION FACT TACTICS

Multiplication facts can be learned in several ways. The following options reflect the learning styles (AVK) found in 1011 H.
Note. Student teams can learn and present these tactics to the class.

1* Singing
Verbal learners enjoy chanting the facts and singing a song - or a rap - to memorize them. Or. Using flash cards, they sing them to their study partner - dramatically, of course. (As this is a noisy tactic, check to see whether a nearby class is in their room. ;))

2* Flash Cards
Students make and decorate flash cards. To practice, they put the ones they know in a pile and practice the others with their math partner.
Note. Cards with the multiplication facts already written on them are handed out to be decorated.

3* Fingers X5
Multiplying with 5's is based on counting by 5's as taught in the lower grades. To introduce the concept, write on the board 5x3. Hold up 3 fingers. Have the children count by 5s as you touch each finger. Write 3x5 = 15.

4* Doubles

Times '2' is the same as 'double 2' which the children chanted in the lower grades. To review, write on the board,

$$1+1 = 2 \qquad 2+2 = 4 \qquad 3+3 = 6$$

Write the multiplication fact underneath. Ask the students to identify the pattern. (The number x 2.) math teams write this pattern up to 9x2.

$$1+1 = 2 \qquad 2+2 = 4 \qquad 3+3 = 6$$

$$1x2=2 \qquad 2x2=4 \qquad 3x2=6$$

5* Times 9

Multiplying by 9 produces a pattern of its own. For instance, adding the 2 digits in the product, adds up to 9. 9X5 = 45 and 4+5=9
(Except for multiplying by '0' which is always '0.')

After students list the X9 facts, challenge the math teams to find other X9 patterns.

6* Grids

Creating a grid for a multiplication fact shows an analysis of the fact.

Using large graph paper, students outline the rows and columns for the facts. To show the answer, they put the numbers in counting order in the boxes. Hmm. I wonder if the children can shut their eyes, feel the shape, and recall the fact?

The numbers at the end of each row shows how to count with that fact. 3x7 counts by 7, 14, 21.
This grid is for 3X7.

Columns... 7

1	2	3	4	5	6	7
8	9	10	11	12	13	14
15	16	17	18	19	20	21

Rows ...
3

7* Multiplication is found by addition
4x3 morphs into adding the number 4 three times.
4+4+4 = 8+4 = 12   Bingo chips prove this fact.

8* Split fact
This process uses vertical multiplication. To identify a large multiplication fact, split the bottom number (called multiplicand) into two smaller numbers with one of them X5.

Multiply the 2 small facts, then add their answers (called a product) to find the final product.

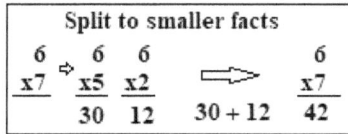

Split to smaller facts					
6	6	6			6
x7 ⇨	x5	x2	⇒		x7
	30	12	30 + 12		42

Summary
By learning options for finding facts and practicing them, memorization happens. Immediate recall saves time.

As a backup for identifying facts above 6X6, consider the finger multiplication technique in the next lesson.

The way is long if one follows precepts, but short…
if one follows patterns.
Lucius Annaeus Seneca

1006.D 1910 FINGER MULTIPLICATION
Note. Using fingers to multiply eventually morphs into memory as just thinking about multiplying 2 fingers recalls the fact.

Story

Digging through a box of old books, my Aunt Jeanne finds a 1910 math book she used in school. What intrigues most me in her math book is using fingers to multiply math facts X6 and higher. Here's how it is done.

1* Turn the hands so the palms are facing toward the face. Thumbs are at the top.

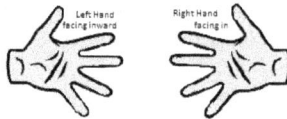

2* Number the fingers. Start with the pinkies as 6 and finish with the thumbs as 10

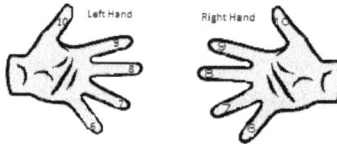

Let's multiply 7 x 7.
3* Touch the two 7 fingers. (ring fingers)

4* Count the touching fingers by ten. Continue counting by ten on the fingers below the touching fingers.

Write down 40.

5* Next, look at the fingers *above* the touching fingers.

On the *left hand* are *3 fingers*. (middle, index, thumb).
On the *right hand* are *3 fingers*. (middle, index, thumb).

6* Multiply 3 x 3 = 9
*7 Add 40 + 9 = 49   7x7 = 49

I have no idea why this works, but congratulations to the mathematical genius who figured it out.

Summary
With practice, a 7th grader quickly uses her fingers to figure out the times facts above 6x6. When a fact is forgotten during math class, she uses her backup method. Eventually, just starting to touch her fingers, she recalls the answer. And that is the purpose of finger multiplication - to use it until the multiplication fact is recalled automatically.

> *For the things of this world cannot be made known without*
> *a knowledge of mathematics.*
> Roger Bacon

1006.E FIGURING FORMULAS
The goal of Tom's tutoring sessions is to discover formulas for geometry. To his amazement, they match the formulas his teacher teaches in his math class.

Given a 3 dimensional shoe box, Tom is asked, "What is the total area of the sides?" He recalls that to find the area of a rectangle, the length is multiplied by the width.   L x W

Examining the box, Tom discovers there are 6 sides or '6 areas,' and the opposite sides are the same. Finding the area of 1 side, he can double the answer to find the 2 sides.

Create a formula.
Tom draws a 3-D box. He labels the edges with letters.

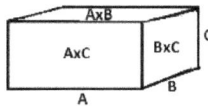

Finding formulas for the area of a box.

$$2(AxB) + 2(BxC) = 2(AxC) = \text{area of box}$$

Using the letters, Tom writes the formula for the area on each side. (6 sides) Writing a number sentence for the sum of all 6 sides shows, he sees that 2 sides match.

$$AxB + AxB + BxC + BxC + AxC + AxC$$

Tom realizes that because there are doubles, he can multiply a side by 2.
$$2x (AxB) + 2x (BxC) + 2x (AxC)$$

Measuring the edges of the box and substituting the numbers in his formula, Tom finds the area of the box.
'A' measures 12 inches. 'B' measures 6 inches. 'C' measures 5 inches.
$$2x (12x6) + 2x (6x5) + 2x (12x5)$$
$$2x72 + 2x30 + 2x60 =$$
$$324$$

Summary
Math formulas are often memorized, applied on the test, and quickly forgotten. Through Tom's analysis to discover a math formula, he understands how he got the formula. If forgotten, he can rediscover it.

Today's scientists have substituted mathematics for experiments, and they wander off equation
through equation, and eventually build a structure
which has no relation to reality.
Nicola Tesla

1006.F COINS AND ALGEBRA
Goal: The 1st graders are introduced to the names of coins, and then taught how combine them to make a dollar.

Substituting letters for the names of the coins makes it easier to write money sentences. During the 1st part of the math session, key ideas are explained. Once the activity is under way, the children are so involved that no one notices when it is time for lunch!

Introduce coins
Sets of coins are placed into baggies labeled 'A' 'B' 'C' etc. Each group of 4 children is assigned a bag of coins. To provide ownership, their names are put on a slip of paper which is put in the baggie. By counting their coins at the beginning and end of class, stress about losing coins is reduced. The 6-year-olds are excited to use real coins.
Bag: 10p, 10n, 10d, and 4q = 34 coins

Part 1 Introduce coin names and basic algebra.
TEACHER "Who knows four coins that add up to $1?"
STUDENT "Four quarters."
On the board, write the number sentence, 'Four quarters equals one dollar.'
TEACHER "This number sentence has a lot of words. How can it be made shorter?"
STUDENT "Use the number 4."
Four' is erased, '4' is written. '4 quarters equals one dollar.'
STUDENT "Use a number 1." '4 quarters equals 1 dollar.'
STUDENT "Use an equal sign."

'4 quarters = 1 dollar.'

Explain to the youngsters that the $ sign means 'dollar.'
The sentence now reads, 4 quarters = $1

TEACHER "Let's make the number sentence even shorter. What 'letter'
can we use to mean 'quarter'?"
STUDENT "Write a 'q'."   4q = $1

TEACHER "Let's read the sentence together. *4q = $1*"
Students read it aloud.
TEACHER "What letters can we use for the other coins?"
The children suggest,   penny = p   dime = d   nickel = n
They are written on the board.
TEACHER "Great job! We now have letters for words."

Part 2
The 2nd part of the lesson focuses on exchanging the coins.

Write on the board. 4q = $1
TEACHER "What 3 coins equal a quarter? Discuss your ideas with your
math group." After a few moments.
TEACHER "What did you find out?"
STUDENT "The quarter is the same as 2 dimes and 1 nickel."
TEACHER "Let's write a new number sentence on the board by taking
out 1 quarter and putting in 2 dimes and 1 nickel."

$$4q = \$1$$
$$3q + 2d + 1n = \$1$$

Note. The 'n' does not actually need a 1 in front of it, but explaining that
algebraic concept to the children is a huge step, so it isn't explained.

The children's eyes light up with excitement as they understand the
process of changing out coins. Record sheets are handed out - one per

group. The children write their names and 'baggie letter' at the top. After they count the coins in the baggies, the coin exchanging begins.

TEACHER "Use the coins to make number sentences that equal one dollar. Put initials by the number sentence to show who thinks of it. Remember to take turns."

At the end of the lesson, their number sentences are written on the board. Red stars on the children's record sheet means their number sentence matches one on the board.

After recounting and collecting the coins, our lesson is over.

TEACHER "This class is awesome! Look at all these coin sentences on the board! Great job! How many do we have? (Count them.) That is a lot! Great thinking!

Summarize
TEACHER "How many of you know the names of the coins? (Hands wave.) How many of you know how to change out the coins to make $1? (Hands wave.) You learned a lot today! Let's clap in a silent circle to celebrate your extraordinary work." Smiles are everywhere as they celebrate their success.

Summary
Because the activity is new and challenging, it's explained in small steps. Group work provides support for deliberate learners. Learning to exchange coins, the 1st graders are better analytical thinkers.

On the way out the door to lunch, one youngster stops to say he had a splendid time. "I'd even skip lunch to write more coin sentences!" What a compliment to the joy of group work.

Never help a child with a task at which
he feels he can succeed.
Maria Montessori

1006.G TIME: ANALOGUE AND DIGITAL

By hanging paper clocks, an analogue clock, a digital clock and outing out time schedules, telling time becomes a necessary skill.

In a 2nd grade classroom, the day's schedule is written vertically on the board. Next to each digital time (such as 12:30 pm) is a paper plate of the 'analogue clock' with the same time. A nearby analogue clock on the wall shows the 'actual' time.

LUNCH   12:30 p.m.

analogue clock

Comparing the paper analogue clock to the wall clock, students quickly recognize when it's almost time to leave for lunch. With lunch money in hand, they line up, and watch the clock. When it's the exact time, out the door they go.

As the teacher sometimes 'forgets' to watch the time, they pay close attention to the schedule. The students remind the teacher when it's time to leave the room for music, art, or gym. And lunch!

When the math unit about time begins, it's quickly learned. Working in teams, the children make clocks of paper plates, draw clock hands on pictures, and write the matching digital times. They are confident and busy.

Sign 'In and Out'
First grade classrooms often have a single bathroom. The youngsters pop in and out all day long. To keep track of visits to the bathroom, a 'sign in

and out chart' with a pencil is set on a nearby desk. When the bathroom is visited, the child records his initials and the times in and out. The students use the analogue clock on the wall to figure out the digital time.

Note. The paper has 3 columns - one for the student's initials and 2 for digital times - going in and coming out of the bathroom. There is no digital clock.

Asking a classmate for help to figure out the digital time is encouraged. A few students realize that if they follow immediately behind someone else, they can use their digital time 'out'.

When a 'messy problem' happens, the next child to use the bathroom is quick to report it. The last child on the chart is sent to find the custodian to help clean up. Very quickly 'messy situations' stop happening.
Note. The custodian is alerted that he might be needed at least once.

Upper grades
Older students use hall passes to go to the restrooms. Signing in and out of the classroom is still required.

Times for the sharpener
Pencil sharpeners are enjoyable, but noisy - especially during a test. A schedule with digital times for sharpening is posted by the sharpener. Returning to the classroom, the line is long, the whirring constant. While class is in session, handheld pencil sharpeners are used over a wastebasket.

Summary
With opportunities to tell time around the classroom, students become automatic 'time tellers.' When the math clock unit starts, we go straight to the harder questions - "How long is it between 4:30 p.m. and 5:00 p.m.?" Math teams figure out the answer with paper clocks.

A man who has not one half his day's work by ten o'clock,
runs a chance of leaving the other half undone.
Emily Bronte

1006.H A PLAN FOR FRACTION CUTOUTS

Teacher's Background

Everything in the Land of Fractions is topsy turvy. First, they have their own language. One digit on top of another, gives the digits new names - numerator and denominator. Adding fractions is possible if the bottom numbers match; but only the top numbers are added or subtracted.

Add Fractions	Multiply Fractions
$\frac{3}{7} + \frac{2}{7} = \frac{5}{7}$	$\frac{1}{2} \times \frac{1}{4} = \frac{1}{8}$

Multiplying is easy. Multiply the numerators, and then multiply the denominators. However, the answer is skewed. It is a smaller answer, not larger! Dividing fractions uses a special reversal rule. The result is a *larger* number! Here is how it works.

Divide Fractions   **Reverse the second fraction.**   **Multiply.**

$\frac{1}{2} \div \frac{1}{8} = 4$ Put in an X. $\frac{1 \times 8 = 8}{2 \times 1 = 2}$

$\frac{1}{2} \times \frac{8}{1} = 4$

The answer is 8 halves, and they = 4 wholes.

Story

Tutoring a student about fractions, he asks. "Why does dividing fractions end up as a whole number?" The challenges is taken. After he leaves, I set up a simple division problem and extrapolated. Here is the explanation.

A simple division problem. 15 divided by 3 It means, how many sets of 3 are in a group of 15? There are 5 sets of 3 in 15.

Then…

$$\frac{1}{2} \div \frac{1}{8} :$$

It means how many 1/8 are in a ½? 4
Yes, 4 is a large number, but it does not mean an amount.
The 4 means how many.

Working with fractions is like being another world.
Like Alice going down the rabbit hole, some things look the same in math, but are not. These fraction charts help explain the 'fraction language.'

$\frac{2}{3}$ numerator / denominator

Explaining a fraction.
The numerator is 2 shaded.
$\frac{2}{3}$
The denominator means 3 equal size pieces.

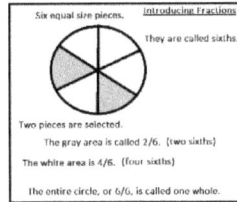

Six equal size pieces. Introducing Fractions
They are called sixths.
Two pieces are selected.
The gray area is called 2/6. (two sixths)
The white area is 4/6. (four sixths)
The entire circle, or 6/6, is called one whole.

Fraction Background for Students

TEACHER "What are fractions? When are they used? What are some examples? How are fractions different from regular numbers?" Students share answers with their math team then with the class.

The bottom number is the denominator. It tells how many equal parts are in the whole. The top number is the numerator. I tells how many parts to color. They are used when a whole is being cut up.

$\frac{2}{3}$

Introduce Fraction Cutouts

TEACHER "Today, each of you will color and cut out a set of fractions. Read the Fraction Plan Sheet with your math partner. After you ask questions about the plan, we will begin.." Hand out the plan sheet for cutting out fractions. After reviewing the plan sheet, students ask questions, then follow the directions.

The Plan
How To Make Fractions

Purpose
Make a set of different size fractions using the same size whole.

Materials
one inch graph paper   scissors   crayons   paper clips
black fine-tipped marker   size 10 envelope   ruler Fraction Plan Sheet pencil

Step 1. Gather the materials.
Step 2. Draw and cut out eight 4-by-6 rectangles.
Step 3. Label one rectangle '1 whole.'
Step 4. Draw lines on each rectangle to show the fraction sizes.
Step 5. With the black tip pen, label each fraction piece 'vertically.' Print big!

Step 6. Use the color list to color the fractions.
Step 7. Cut out the fractions.

Step 8. Put your initials on the back of each piece.
Step 9. Put your name on the envelope.
Step 10. Paper clip the matching fractions, then put them in the envelope. Put the envelope in a safe place.
Step 11. What might go wrong? Add notes to your plan sheet to avoid problems.

1 whole

$\frac{1}{2}$ $\frac{1}{2}$

$\frac{1}{3}$ $\frac{1}{3}$ $\frac{1}{3}$

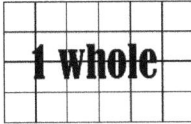

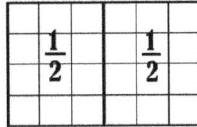

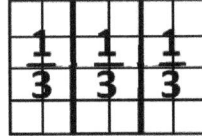

Fraction Color List		
Whole	1	Red
Half	$\frac{1}{2}$	Orange
Third	$\frac{1}{3}$	Yellow
Fourth	$\frac{1}{4}$	Green
Sixth	$\frac{1}{6}$	Light Blue
Eighth	$\frac{1}{8}$	Light Purple
Twelth	$\frac{1}{12}$	Pink
Twenty-·fourth	$\frac{1}{24}$	Brown

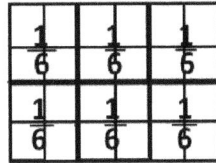

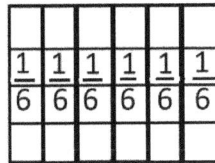

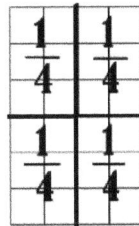

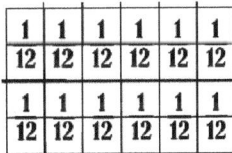

$\frac{1}{8}$ $\frac{1}{8}$ $\frac{1}{8}$ $\frac{1}{8}$
$\frac{1}{8}$ $\frac{1}{8}$ $\frac{1}{8}$ $\frac{1}{8}$

$\frac{1}{6}$ $\frac{1}{6}$ $\frac{1}{6}$
$\frac{1}{6}$ $\frac{1}{6}$ $\frac{1}{6}$

$\frac{1}{6}$ $\frac{1}{6}$ $\frac{1}{6}$ $\frac{1}{6}$ $\frac{1}{6}$ $\frac{1}{6}$

$\frac{1}{4}$ $\frac{1}{4}$
$\frac{1}{4}$ $\frac{1}{4}$

$\frac{1}{12}$ $\frac{1}{12}$ $\frac{1}{12}$ $\frac{1}{12}$ $\frac{1}{12}$ $\frac{1}{12}$
$\frac{1}{12}$ $\frac{1}{12}$ $\frac{1}{12}$ $\frac{1}{12}$ $\frac{1}{12}$ $\frac{1}{12}$

Summary
This hands-on activity proves to students that fractions are a part of a whole. Using the same size 'whole' allows the fraction pieces be compared. Why?

An analogy
If you are given half of an 8 inch pizza, and your friend is given half of a 16 inch pizza, both of you have half. But who eats the bigger slice? For

each of you to have the same size pizza slice, the half must be from the same size whole. Compare fractions from the same whole.

> *If I were beginning my studies, I would follow the advice*
> *of Plato and start with mathematics.*
> Galileo Galilei

1006.I COMPARE FRACTIONS
Rule. To compare 2 fractions, they must be from the same size whole. These 4 lessons define fraction sizes and identify fraction equivalents. $1/2 = 2/4$

Mini-Assignments
TEACHER "Take out your fractions. Put your name and date on your record sheet.

*Lesson 1. Large to small
TEACHER "Choose one fraction piece from each size pile. Arrange the fraction pieces from *large to small*. On your record sheet, list the fractions in order. Write the fractions vertically. Label the list Large to Small."
TEACHER "What happens to the numerators as the fraction sizes get smaller?
STUDENT "The numerators stay a '1.'"
TEACHER "What happens to the denominators as the fraction sizes get smaller?
STUDENT The denominators get larger."
TEACHER "With your math team, write a sentence to explain why the denominators get larger."
STUDENT "The denominators get larger when there are more fraction pieces."

*Lesson 2. Small to large
Large to small

TEACHER "Choose one fraction piece from each size pile. Arrange the fraction pieces from *small to large*. Record them in order on your record sheet. Label the list small to large.'
(Ask the questions from Lesson 1.)

*Lesson 3. Equivalent fractions
TEACHER "Find *two equal size* pieces that fit on top of *one* piece. Write the fraction sentence. These are called equivalent fractions because they are equal in size."
STUDENT "We fit two ¼ on top of ½ , so we write…"

Equivalent Fractions

$$\frac{2}{4} = \frac{1}{2}$$

TEACHER "Use your fractions to find more."

*Lesson 4. Other equivalents
TEACHER "What fractions have *more than two* identical fractions that fit on top of it?"
STUDENT "4 of the 1/8 fit on top of one half."
TEACHER "This time the numerator is 4. Why?"
STUDENT "Because 4 fraction pieces were used."

Equivalent Fractions
$\frac{4}{8} = \frac{1}{2}$

TEACHER "Compare your equivalent fractions with other study teams."

*Lesson 5. Prove 2 fractions are equivalent

TEACHER "To prove 2 fractions are equivalent, multiply the opposite numerator and denominator. If the products are equal, the 2 fractions are equivalent. With your math partner, identify more examples."

Proof for Equivalent Fractions

$$\frac{3}{6} \diagdown\diagup \frac{1}{2}$$

$$3 \times 2 = 6 \times 1$$
$$6 = 6$$

STUDENTS The class shares results by drawing and explaining their proofs at the board.

Summary
Ask the math teams to answer these questions. The class then shares their answers.

*What does a denominator tell us?

It tells *how many equal pieces* are in the *whole.*

*What does a numerator tell us?

[It tells *how many we have of equal size 'pieces'* of the same whole.]

*What do fractions show when they stack perfectly on top of each other?

[*They show they are equivalent fractions.]*

*What happens to fraction sizes when the denominators get bigger?"

[*If the numerators stay the same, the fraction pieces get smaller.]*

*What happens to fraction sizes when the denominators get smaller?"

[*If the numerators stay the same, the fraction pieces get bigger.]*

TEACHER "If you want a big piece of pizza, what's the best number of people to share with? With your team partner, draw pictures to prove this fact."

STUDENT "One other person is best because we each get half."

TEACHER "Let's have a math team prove this at the board."

The greatest sign of success for a teacher…
is to be able to say,
"The children are now working
as though I did not exist."
Maria Montessori

1006.J MEASURE A TREE'S HEIGHT

The multiplication rule that proves equivalent fractions is used here.
Note. The students must be able to measure with rulers and/or yardsticks.
Calculators are needed.

OVERVIEW OF THE PROCESS

A Tree Height Note. Round up the measurements
Step 1. Each child measures his/her height in inches.
Step 2. Each child measures his/her shadow in inches.
Step 3. Each team measures a tree's shadow in inches.
Step 4. After writing the equivalent fractions, students use a calculator to 'cross multiply and divide.'
The division answer is the height of the tree.

THE DETAILS OF THE PROCESS

TEACHER "Let's review how to find a missing number in two equivalent fractions." Show this chart on the overhead. Teams discuss the process.

Equivalent Fractions

$$\frac{1}{3} = \frac{?}{12}$$

We know 1 x 12 = 12
What number is multiplied
by 3, so the answer is 12?
3 x 4 = 12
The missing number is 4.

TEACHER "How can we measure the height of a tree?"
STUDENT "Use a tall ladder…etc."

TEACHER "Let's use our formula for equivalent fractions to find the height of a tree."

$$\frac{\text{person's height}}{\text{person's shadow}} = \frac{\text{tree's height } X}{\text{tree's shadow}}$$

TEACHER "To find the height of the tree, we need 3 measurements to build 2 equivalent fractions.
'X' will be the 'unknown' height of the tree.

TEACHER "Which of these numbers are measured easily?
STUDENT "Our height, our shadow length, and the tree's shadow length."
TEACHER "Yes. Measure them, then put the 3 numbers into the formula. Use your calculator to find the 4th number.

Note. This activity is best done near twelve noon when shadows are the shortest. In early morning or late afternoon, tree shadows may reach 150 feet!

Tree Height ... number example
Feet become inches by multiplying by 12. If there are extra inches. add them to the total/product.

Person's height. 5 feet or 60 inches
Person's shadow. 4 feet or 48 inches
Tree's shadow..32 feet or 384 inches

See the equivalent fraction below. The numbers are big!
'X' is the tree's height which is unknown.

Use calculators
Multiply the opposite numerator and denominator.
60 x 384 = 23,040 inches
Then divide it by the denominator 48 to find the numerator.

23,404 inches is the tree's height!

Divide by 12 to find the number of feet. The tree is 40 feet tall.
Note. If the numbers do not divide evenly, stop at the decimal point.

$$\frac{60}{48} = \frac{X}{384}$$

48X = 60x384

48X = 23,040

23,040 divided by
48 = 480 inches

To find feet,divide by 12 inches.

Tree is 40 feet tall!

Summary
Applying the multiplication rule for equivalent fractions to measure tree heights is an amazing application. It's equivalent fractions 'on steroids.'

The best time to plant a tree is 25 years ago.
The second best time to plant a tree is today.
Eliud Kipchoge

CHAPTER 6 IN CONCLUSION
DISCOVER MATH

Whether simple or complex math, the essence of learning is discovery. Children who figure out math basics, its rules and formulas, remember and understand them longer. Dive in deeply to break a problem into its parts... examine them for unique patterns ... analyze rules and find the answer... This imprints long term memory.

Story
The soon-to-be professor forgets his packet of formulas for his final PhD math exam. (An absent minded professor perhaps?) With no time to return home, he asks for and is granted permission ' to invent' his own

formulas. "As long as they work," says his Math Professor. They do. The mathematical meaning behind the formulas is thoroughly understood.

"On two occasions I have been asked,
"I pray, Mr. Babbage, if you put into your machine
wrong numbers,
will the right answers come out?"
I am not able to comprehend the kind of confusion of ideas
that could provoke such a question."
Charles Babbage

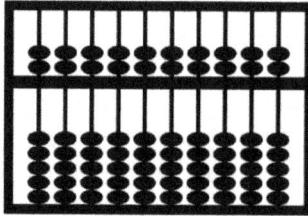

Chapter 7
Investigate Science

Observe, identify a hypothesis, test

Topics
A. Compare Leaves   B. Count Leaves   C. Moth and Bugs
D. Bat, Snake, Fish   E. Light Bulbs   F. Measure Bubbles
G. Analyze Food Coloring   H. Observe Pendulums
I. Ants and Original Research   J. Arctic Bear

Introduction
Systematic thinking is necessary to plan and explore a science activity. Begin with observation, analyze implications, then perform the investigation and compare to the original hypothesis. These skills carry over to understanding new situations, and supports students' success in life.

If time is short, include one student-centered science activity every two weeks to develop 'scientific thinkers.' A science activity includes keen observation, specific materials, investigative questions, a detailed plan, and predictions or hypotheses. Examining the results includes a process review and updates.

What an amazing skill to give a student during their school career - *systematic thinking*. As a lifelong skill, many mistakes are avoided by proper thinking before, during, and after an event.

Writing reports to explain science investigations requires information, specific details, and implications based on reasoning. Science activities builds better thinkers and writers and learners. It is an important subject in the curriculum.

Nothing has such power to broaden the mind as the ability
to investigate systematically and truly
all which comes under one's observation in life.
Marcus Aurelius

1007.A ARE ALL THE LEAVES ON ONE TREE ALIKE?

A careful observation of plants and animals, encourages young people to appreciate Nature. These 2 lessons are based on observing leaves. Related writing activities are at the end of this lesson.
1005.I FROM PHOTOS TO POETRY
1005.J SEASONS AND HAIKU

Set up
Gather leaves from *the same tree*; collect a few more than the number of children in the class. Press them between absorbent tissues in a large book. After 2 or 3 days, the leaves are dry and nicely flattened.

Spread the leaves on a tray and let each child choose one. With extra leaves, the last child has a choice. Give the class a few moments to study their leaf.

TEACHER "Describe your leaf to your team partner."
STUDENTS "It has rounded edges...4 veins... a long stem piece. One part is missing. It feels rough... smooth... bumpy.'"
TEACHER "What makes your leaf different from other leaves?"
STUDENTS "The veins have a different pattern. The edges, colors, and sizes are different."
TEACHER "Examine it one more time to be sure you know your leaf."

Collect the leaves on the tray. Spread them out on a large table or counter so every leaf is clearly visible. Tell the class to stand so all can see the leaves. Taller students look over the shoulders of shorter students. After a minute of looking for their leaf, tell them to carefully pick up their leaf. To their happy surprise, everyone picks up their own leaf.

TEACHER "How do you know it's your leaf?"
STUDENTS "Mine has a hole in it. One of the edges is broken. The stem is thicker than other leaves."
TEACHER "Since all these leaves are from the same tree, why do they look different?"
STUDENT "Bugs chew it... different amounts of sunlight...from a different part of the tree....gets more rain."

Writing activity
Question. "What words describe a leaf and its experiences?" As students brainstorm vocabulary words, record them on the board. Choose, then explain the criteria for one of the following assignments.

Options
- Write a detailed description of the leaf. Include size, texture, and color. Use different viewpoints such as told by a bird, insect, or raindrop.
- Write a biography from the time the leaf buds to the time it floats off the tree - or whirls away in the wind. Include a timeline from Chapter 11.
- Write a letter of advice from the tree to the leaf. Include a chart for details. Use Chapter 11.
1011.G 2-D GRAPHIC DESIGNS

Leaf rubbing
Place a sheet of thin plain white paper over a leaf. Peel the paper off a crayon and use its side to color over the paper until the leaf veins show through. Color in the same direction. The paper and leaf need to be firmly held when doing the edges. This is a grand celebration.
1008.A ARE ALL THE LEAVES ON ONE TREE ALIKE?

Note. Leaf rubbings prevent the leaves from drying, crumpling, and ending up on the floor. Although, the final end of a leaf is, after all, mulch. *Laughter.*

Summary

For the children, examining the leaf to make it their own goes beyond the lesson. For the child to pick up a leaf anywhere and anytime, leads to thinking of its history, its name, and perhaps even its future. The environment comes closer to the childlike heart. Their love embraces all of Nature.

> *I said to the almond tree, speak to me of God,*
> *and the almond tree blossomed.*
> Nikos Kazantzakis

1007.B HOW MANY LEAVES ON A TREE?

A tree in full leaf is an awesome sight. This estimation activity counts into the hundreds and thousands.

How do we count the leaves on a tree? Team and a class discussion will uncover that by counting a few, estimation does the rest.

Going outside with a clipboard, pencil, and paper, each team finds a tree. The students count the number of leaves in a small area of the branches. Standing back to see the whole tree, they estimate how many of the 'small areas' there are. Multiplying the 2 numbers is the estimate of the number of the tree's leaves. Anyone who finishes early can repeat the counting or count another tree's leaves.

If there are 75 leaves in the small area, and 52 small areas, multiply 75 x 52. The estimate is 3900 leaves on the tree.

Students compare their tree count with students who counted the same tree.

Class discussion
TEACHER "When teams use the same tree, why are answers different?"

STUDENTS "We can't see all the leaves. We overlap or leave out areas. Estimates aren't exact."

Summary

Estimates are 'implication thinking.' If this, then that. Scientists estimate time, number, and distance. How long did this mountain take to form? How long ago did dinosaurs live? How far away is the next planet? Although the numbers scientists tell us seem to be carved in stone, scientists have different answers just as the students do. The method of analysis, who does it, and when impacts the answers.

> *Autumn is a second Spring when very leaf is a flower.*
> Albert Camus

1007.C MOTH AND BUG VISITORS
Story
Suddenly a 6-inch wide brown and yellow moth fluttered out of its hiding place and onto the whiteboard. The 1st graders squealed in delight. "Look! A butterfly! What's it doing here?" This begins an impromptu science lesson.

TEACHER "It looks like butterfly, but it's called a moth. I'll sketch their differences. A butterfly rests with its wings closed. This is a moth because it rests with its wings open. Moths usually come out at night, butterflies in the day. Close up, the moth's antennae are feathery looking; the butterfly's antennae are smooth. Antennae are used to smell flowers. Then, the insect drinks the nectar.

STUDENTS "What are those large spots? They look like eyes."
TEACHER "Why do you think they look like eyes?"
STUDENTS "To scare away its enemies!"
TEACHER "You're right. Let's take it outside, so it can hide until dark."

Coaxing the moth into a jar with a piece of paper, we carry it outside to the nearby trees. Giving the jar a gentle shake, the moth falls to the ground. Using the paper, it is scooted it under a bush. "There's no point in saving the moth's life only to leave it out in the open for a bird to eat. Large eye spots or not, a hungry bird eats moths."

Returning to the classroom, we talk about caring for insects and animals and why we let them go. The insect lesson is over. We return to our school lessons.

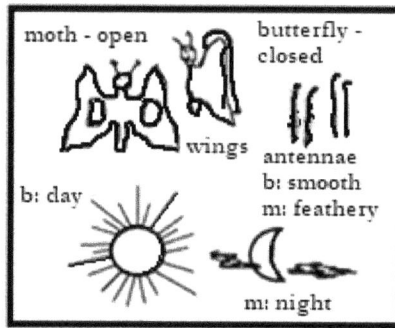

Summary
Children are often fascinated by bugs. Some teachers are not. Assign a student 'Bug Catcher' to support the theme of 'catch and release,. This avoids the 'yuck' aspect for an adult.

> *Nature will bear the closest inspection.*
> *She invites us to lay our eye level with her smallest leaf,*
> *and take an insect view of its plain.*
> Henry David Thoreau

1007.D A BAT. A SNAKE. THE FISH.
The following 3 stories are examples of Nature's wildlife in the classroom of long ago. In today's classrooms, a lost ladybug may not welcomed, much less a garter snake.

The Snake

For me, anything that explains Nature is a lesson. In our 2nd grade classroom, a classroom terrarium is built with small rocks and green plants. A garter snake caught outside makes it complete. A piece plastic wrap is stretched over the top. The greenery provides oxygen. The children enjoy watching the snake sleep and eat the bugs we give him.

One morning when I enter the classroom, the snake is standing tall with its tail wriggling behind. The problem? He is scooting across my desk. It suddenly seems the right time to take it back to its natural habitat. After the children arrive, we escort the little one outside to the nearest trees. Placed under a bush, we wish it well.

The Bat

Due to a lack of a science curriculum, teaching is day by day. A new idea is always welcome. One morning, a student brought one.

A 5th grade boy carries a small box into the room. Inside is a bat, the kind that fly. With the help of the custodian, we find a large box the size of a refrigerator. Cutting a hole in the side, plastic wrapping is taped over it. A branch inside gives the little fellow a place to hang.

The morning classes love seeing a bat up close. Seeing bats in their neighborhoods, they share their observations. Discussions range from their habitats to sleep patterns to food sources to 'bat radar.'

Everything changed at lunch when the principal is informed that we have a bat in the classroom. "Bats have diseases," he says. "The bat must leave now." The student who brought it, takes it home right away. The custodian removes the box.

The bat lesson turns out to be a lesson for me. Future wild animals are borrowed from the high school science teachers who tame and vet them for diseases and friendly behavior. From raccoons to a chinchilla our science classes learned about animals firsthand.

The Fish
A delightful substitute takes over my 5th grade class while I'm on leave. Every night, we call each other to review the lesson plans.

About the fish. One morning, the little fellows are found floating on top of the water. The sub takes them away before the students arrive. We couldn't figure out what happened.

Upon my return, a student cheerfully informs me that he kept an eye on the fish. "Every time the little red light went on, I adjusted the thermometer until the light went out." I did not tell him that adjusting the light to go off meant the water is heated higher. Some things teachers do not tell children.

Summary
Bug, bird, and leaf identification books and a discussion time for sharing Nature facts, keep students engaged in their world. With secondary and primary research, science is connected to the world outside the schoolroom.

> *Bats drink on the wing like swallows by sipping the surface*
> *as they play over pools and streams.*
> Gilbert White

Science Investigations
The following 4 science lessons are based on the same 'plan format.' In each case, the plans are discussed by the students, questions are asked and answered, and then the activity begins.

 If the students are experienced in following a plan, teacher review about a plan is skipped.

1011.A REDUCE PROBLEMS. PLAN EVERYTHING

```
+---------------------------------+
|           A Plan                |
|                                 |
| 1. Set the purpose.             |
| 2. Explain the details.         |
| 3. List the materials.          |
| 4. Identify the steps.          |
| 5. Review and make              |
| corrections and addtions.       |
+---------------------------------+
```

1007.E BULBS AND BATTERIES

This is a 2 day investigation with 5 students. Each student is given a mini light bulb, a piece of aluminum foil, and a size D battery. The investigation question is, "How does a battery make a light bulb light up? Note. The bulbs were found in a big box store.

TEACHER "Each of you have a piece of foil, a small light bulb, and a size D (1.5 volt) battery. Your goal is to make the bulb light up. Each time you investigate a different combination of foil, bulb, and battery, draw a picture of your set up. Write down why you think the setup works or does not work."

Day 1

At the end of the 1st class session, students choose one of their sketches to draw on the board. They explain their drawing and why it works or doesn't work. Group members ask questions.

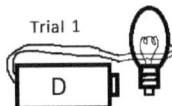
Trial 1

Examples
Student. "I put the foil on the bulb. I thought the electricity would go

through the glass. It did not light up. I think the electricity couldn't go through the glass."

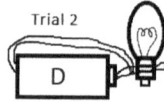
Trial 2

Student. "I connected 2 pieces of foil to both ends of the battery and to the screw part. I thought electricity would go inside. I think it didn't light up because the electricity got stuck in the same place."

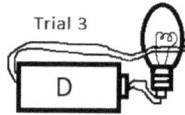
Trial 3

Student. "I put one piece of foil on the battery's flat end and on the glass. I put a second piece of foil on the other end of the battery and then to the bottom of the bulb. I thought the electricity needed both ends of the battery to touch the bulb. I think it didn't light up because the glass stopped the electricity from getting inside."

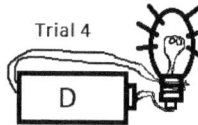
Trial 4

Day 2

The 2nd day brought success.

Student. "My bulb lit up! I put a foil piece on the flat end of the battery and then to the screw part of the bulb. I put another piece of foil from the tip of the battery to the bottom tip of the bulb. I did this because I saw the bulb's screw part was different at the bottom. I thought maybe each bulb part connected to the battery differently. I think it lit up because the electricity went inside the bulb."

After a child lights the bulb, everyone pays close attention to the drawing and explanation. They make their bulbs light up, too. One child discovers that the bulb lights up even when the foil on the ends of the battery is reversed,

Discussion
TEACHER "What part of the bulb lit up?"
STUDENT "The wire inside."
TEACHER "How do you think it is connected to the bottom of the bulb?"
STUDENT "One side of the wire connects to the screw part, the other to the bottom tip."

At this point, students understand that electricity needs a *path* for the electricity to go *in and out* of the bulb.

TEACHER "How does electricity make the bulb light? Rub your hands together, and they get warm. Rubbing 2 sticks together makes enough heat to start the twigs on fire. The electricity goes through the wire inside. Because it's made of a different metal, the electricity pushes harder. The friction makes it hot enough to light up."

History
Thomas Edison, who produced 'the light of the future' is the 1st inventor to make a long lasting light bulb. Highly intelligent technicians come from across the U.S. and Europe to Edison's workshop. Under his directions, the 'muckers' create thousands of combinations of metals, glass, and gases in an effort to create a bulb that lit up, stayed lit - and didn't explode!

Check https://www.livescience.com/43424-who-invented-the-light-bulb.html for more details. Scientists around the world were also working to invent a light bulb.

Summary
Students need two 45 minute sessions to explore their options in making the bulb light. Investigating independently means trial and error. Sharing their results at the end of the first day clarifies what is happening and the possible reasons. Hearing about the failed attempts, spurs them to try new setups.

1007.F MEASURE BUBBLES

The children love this activity because it includes 'playing' with water and soap. The teacher appreciates the clean desks.

Overview
To investigate water tension, students blow soap bubbles and measure the circles of the popped bubbles. Based on observation, they predict when the bubbles will pop. To record bubble sizes, a chart is used.

Name_____   Date_____

Bubble Record Sheet

Bubble	Amount of Water	Amount of Soap	Size of Popped Bubble
1			
2			
3			
4			
5			
Notes	1/4 teaspoon of glycerin was added to the soap mixture.		

Sample Bubble Chart

Logical reasoning and predicting with an activity and observation makes this a multifaceted lesson. The clean desks complement the daily classroom cleaning.
1009.A ONE MINUTE TO A CLEAN CLASSROOM

Note. As the plan is reviewed on the smart board or overhead, students 'imagine' the activity. Seeing it mentally, it's easier to suggest additions and corrections. Their additions are written on the plan in a different color. On the plan below, student additions are printed in BLOCK LETTERS.

The Plan
Investigate Soap Bubbles

*Purpose. To identify the best way to blow a large soap bubble and predict when it will pop.

*Overview
Use liquid soap mixed in water to blow bubbles. Use rulers to measure the bubble's 'pop size,' and record the results on a chart.

*Materials. A record sheet for recording bubble sizes, centimeter ruler, pencils, dish soap, water, straws.
STUDENTS ADD: EYE DROPPERS PAPER TOWELS, PAPER CUP, TEASPOON, DESKS.

*Steps
1. Gather materials.

2. Make bubble soap.
Discussion. How can we be sure we all have the same mixture to investigate?
STUDENTS ADD: FILL THE PAPER CUP HALFWAY WITH WATER. USE THE EYEDROPPER TO ADD 5 DROPS OF DISH SOAP.

3. Pour bubble mixture on the desk. Discussion. How much?
PUT 4 TEASPOONS OF THE BUBBLE MIXTURE ON THE DESK.

4. Slowly blow a bubble. Discussion. How?
DIP THE END OF THE STRAW IN THE MIXTURE. BLOW A BUBBLE UNTIL IT POPS.
5. Measure the 'pop.' Discussion. How?

MEASURE THROUGH THE MIDDLE OF THE 'POP CIRCLE' WITH THE RULER.

6. Record the bubble size. ON THE CHART

7. Clean up.
CLEAN UP WITH PAPER TOWELS. THROW THEM AWAY IN THE TRASH.

8. Problems or omissions. What might go wrong? What new details are added to the plan to take care of the problem? [See the additions in the block lettering above.]

After the plan is clarified and corrected, students gather their materials and blow bubbles. During the activity, the children cheerfully call out suggestions such as 'Blow slowly for a bigger bubble,' and predict when it will pop, 'The colors are starting to change.'

Summary
A written plan leads to an activity's success. Identifying problems and their solutions before starting the activity is a key component to executing a successful plan.

The best laid plans of mice and men do often go awry.
Robert Burns

...unless - problems and solutions are identified first!

1007.G WHAT COLORS MAKE FOOD COLORING?
A small group of 3rd graders do this investigation as an enrichment activity. To introduce the concept of color mixing, we talk about combining basic colors in art class, such as red mixed with blue makes purple.

'Osmosis' is introduced - 'whereby a liquid moves from a saturated situation [the glass of water] to a non-saturated situation [the dry paper towel.]' Merriam – Webster Dictionary
For the children, the definition is, 'Liquids like to find empty spaces.'

Note. Osmosis defies gravity because it travels *up a tree* to its leaves. How? After water evaporates from the top leaves, there are spaces inside the leaf. Water from the branch fills in the leaf spaces. The branch spaces get water from the tree trunk which receives water from the roots which comes from the ground. This process makes an interesting diagram.

Another investigation
Compare the water drop 'jump' to a paper towel with ripped edges and one with flat edges. (An editor contributed this idea.)

The plan below is dictated by the students. Problems are discussed and solutions added as it is written. It takes a full class session to write it.

Based on 'reverse engineering,' the goal is to 'undo the food coloring' to discover what colors are used to make it. Children who take apart toys and clocks are familiar with this process as are their parents.

The Plan
Food Coloring Investigation

*Purpose. To identify the colors used to make food coloring.

*Overview
Food coloring is added to glasses of water. Paper towel strips absorb the water by osmosis. The results show the colors.

*Materials
Paper towels, 6 bottles of different food coloring, 6 glasses, water, tape,

ruler, spoon, scissors, black marker, paper, pencils, spoon or stir stick, a place to set the glasses on.

Steps
1. Gather materials.
2. Fill the glasses with the same amount of water.
3. Number each glass with the marker, then set them on the counter against the wall.
4. Measure and cut 6 equal size narrow strips of paper towel.
For instance, 1 ½ x 8 inches.
5. Number each strip to match the glass.
6. Add 5 drops of food coloring to each glass and stir.
7. Tape strips to the wall so they hang at the same level in each glass.
8. Draw a sketch of the glass and paper strip. Label.
9. Predict what will happen to the colors. Color a picture to predict the strips' colors.
10. Clean up.

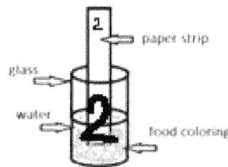

Wait 24 hours. .
11. Take the paper towel strips out of the glasses and set them to dry on a clean paper towel.
12. When dry, compare the strips to the drawings. Students compare their results, then discuss why.

Discussion
What colors were in each strip? How much of the color? Why? If we set up a new investigation, what should we do differently. Why?

Summary
A true science 'experiment' *has never been done before*. Elon Musk, Isaac Newton, and Alxander Graham Bell are examples those who set up experiments. An *investigation* is based on a previously proved experiment. The answer is known, it is being proved.

> *I have steadily endeavored to keep my mind free*
> *so as to give up any hypothesis, however much beloved*
> *(and I cannot resist forming one on every subject),*
> *as soon as the facts are shown to be opposed to it.*
> Charles Darwin

1007.H SWINGING PENDULUMS

History
The Chinese used swinging pendulums to detect earthquakes in 100 AD. In 1602, Galileo investigated the movement of the pendulum and applied it to keeping time. In 1658, Christian Huygen's pendulum clock became the world's first standard timekeeper and is used for over 270 years. (Those are the grandfather clocks we have today.) The quartz clock replaced the pendulum clock in the 1900's. Due to the popularity of the digital clocks, many people today cannot read an analogue clock.

An interested student can use secondary research to share new information with the class.

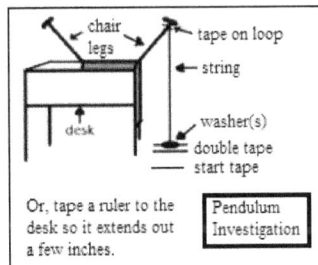

~ 165 ~

The Plan
An Investigation of a Pendulum

The diagram above shows how to set a chair on a desk and attach the string for a pendulum. Or, tape a ruler so it sticks out from the desk. Tie a loop, and hang it at the end.

Purpose
Students observe a pendulum to find out how seconds and swings relate.

*Materials. (for teams of 2 students)
masking tape, string, ruler or yardstick, scissors, 6 metal washers of the same size and weight, a record sheet and pencil, a desk and chair (or a long stick and book), a time piece with a second hand.

*Steps.
1. Set the chair on the desk so one leg sticks out.
2. Make a loop in the string for hanging it.
3. Tie the washer at the string's bottom.
4. Create a stopping space under the string with 2 pieces of masking tape.
5. Decide how far back the washer will be held before letting go. Put a piece of tape to mark the starting spot.
6. Measure the distance between the letting go point and the first piece of the double tape pieces. Record the distance on the chart.

The Pendulum Swing
A. Hold the washer back to the start tape. Let go.
B. One child counts the number of times the washer swings over the two pieces of tape - *both back and forth*. The other child keeps track of the seconds.
C. The counting stops when the washer swings inside the double tape pieces. Be consistent about the stopping point.
D. Record the number of swings and seconds.

E. Undo the string at the top, and slide on a second washer. Tape the loop again keeping the length of the string the same.
F. Repeat the swings and counting.
G. Continue with a 3rd, 4th and 5th washer.

Discussion Questions
How many swings and seconds happen with the different washers? Did the whole class have the same results? Why? What is the relationship between the swinging with more weights and the number of seconds?

Chart

Pendulum Chart		
Change the number of weights.		
Length of string _____		
Distance of start point from stop point._____		
Number of weights	Seconds to stop	Number of swings
_____	_____	_____
_____	_____	_____
_____	_____	_____
_____	_____	_____
_____	_____	_____
Name _____		Date_____

Summary
As weights increase, a pattern emerges between the number of swings and the number of seconds. The key to valid results? Only one criteria is changed during the investigation This investigation of the number of washers.

Opinion is like a pendulum and obeys the same law.
If it goes past the center of gravity on one side,
it must go a like distance on the other, and it is only
after a certain time that it finds the true point
at which it can remain at rest.
Arthur Schopenhauer

I have not failed.
I just found 10,000 ways that won't work.
Thomas Edison

1007.I ANTS AND ORIGINAL RESEARCH

The foundation of original research is observation and logical interpretations. This original research includes ants means, watch them go about their business, take notes, and draw sketches of their actions and destinations.

Students reports explain ant behaviors which provides a better understanding of Nature and ants. Later, when students read original research, they will know the scientist has 'been there, done that!'

Summary
Investigative research stretches student thinking and individualizes the activity because they are exploring their own questions. Sharing their reports gives a broad picture of ant behaviors.

In questions of science, the authority of a thousand
is not worth the humble reasoning
of a single individual.
Galileo

1007.J THE ARCTIC OR THE POLAR BEAR?

The education course requires teaching a lesson that uses 'brainstorming.' A 5th grade teacher graciously allows me to conduct a review of the Arctic for the students' final test. It is exciting to try a new teaching technique. A review question is identified with lots of answers. Or so it seemed.

The lesson
Introducing myself, we chat a bit.

Note. The first time there is 'chatting' by a visiting teacher, it is anxiously wondered if he would run out of time for the lesson. He later explains that 'chat time' focuses the students on the teacher and makes them receptive to the activity - which then goes faster.

"What will happen to the polar bear if the Arctic temperature goes up 20 degrees?" is written on the board. Student answers include, "He would be hot. His hair would fall out. He would move away." That is it. No more hands wave. The lesson on brainstorming is flubbing. Help is needed.

Glancing at the classroom teacher, he suggests, "What will happen to the *Arctic* if the Arctic temperature goes up 20 degrees?" 'Polar bear' is changed to 'Arctic.' Answers fly! From grass growing to ice floes melting to new animals moving North, to the frozen tundra melting their knowledge of the Arctic proved immense. This is indeed a compliment to their classroom teacher.

Summary
While brainstorming, top achievers challenge themselves to give unique answers while the more deliberate thinkers consider an answer carefully before speaking. Pauses allow time for the class to reflect on the previous answers and think of new ones.
1001.C THE OPEN-ENDED QUESTION - INCREASE ANSWERS

It is better to debate a question without settling it,
than to settle a question without debating it.
Joseph Joubert

CHAPTER 7 IN CONCLUSION
INVESTIGATE SCIENCE

A carefully crafted science activity based on a detailed plan develops systemic thinking. It's easier to incorporate a simple, planned science into the classroom. Yet, plans made in school and performed during recess or at home encourage investigations into the students' world. Between original and secondary research, students learn science.

Story
An 'enrichment loop' happens during the food coloring lesson. As the students are setting up the glasses of water, the teacher reviews the lesson book. Moments later, it's discovered that the students set up not 6, but 12 glasses of water along the counter. The children had made a decision to mix the food coloring to create and investigate new colors.

Science and technology revolutionize our lives,
but memory, tradition and myth frame our response.
Arthur M. Shlesinger

Chapter 8
A Culture's Foundation: Social Studies & History

Begin with the individual, gain the greater good

Topics
A. Democracy B. Petition C. Majority Rule? D. Analyze War
E. Mandan Research F. Exchange Experts G. Roman Empire
H. Market Place I. Schoolhouse J. Famous People
K. Conestoga Wagon

*Those who do not remember the past
are condemned to repeat it.*
George Santayana

Introduction
Civilization is a collective experience from which it is important that we all benefit. Valuable lessons are gleaned from the victories and defeats of the past. Using the past to identify long range implications for today means better decisions. Past successes drive us forward to new triumphs.

A serious drawback to children studying history is that dates, places, people, and events from the past are like a new movie - entertaining, but easily forgotten. For adults with no memory hooks to recall the past, hard won lessons are forgotten over time. Societies and civilization become a merry-go-round of repeated mistakes.

To create a common background with adults and each other, students investigate different perspectives of past events and people. This establishes a base for understanding our nation today. Contrariwise, examining history in light of personal perspectives and preferences skews understanding - as a group of high school students discovered.
1008.F ANALYZE WAR

How do we prepare our students to appreciate history and its impact on today's world? Create immersion experiences based on collaboration. Collecting research and collaborating with others, students gain an appreciation of different viewpoints as they develop their own. The bottom line? They learn compassion and fairness.

Group activities, infused with memorable details, unique comparisons, and different levels of critical thinking, deepen connections to history and build a broad understanding for handling today.

Education is not the filling of a pail,
but the lighting of a fire.
William Butler Yeats

As education dissolves, catastrophes
become more common.
Bruce F. Carter

1008.A DEMOCRACY IN THE CLASSROOM

Democracy is a form of government. In general, the citizens through the House of Representatives have the authority to deliberate and decide legislation - the making of laws. The Senate votes to pass or reject them. The Executive Branch carries out these laws.

Background
Democracy is introduced in a 2nd grade classroom in Endicott-Endwell, NY. From planning field trips to writing permission slips, from money collected for a project to phone calls to schedule school buses, these 7 year old children take on adult roles. When a decision is to be made, it means one person, one vote.

Starry-eyed, it's exciting to teach children to love and participate in their classroom activities as they will someday participate in running their country. It is hoped they will develop into true patriots. As a child, this is a key focus in my schoolrooms from patriotic songs to saying the pledge each morning and respecting the flag.

During the 1st week of school, democracy and responsibility are explained. The students identify the duties of a class president, vice president, secretary, and treasurer. Students are nominated, an election is held with paper ballots as it is easy for them to collect, count, and maintain the privacy of the voter. After the final count, officers are inducted. We are ready! With the officers in charge, class activities are given to the class to plan and execute.

Zoo trip
Using a calendar, the 2nd graders discuss the date and times to go and return. Joey's job as treasurer is to call the zoo and ask for the cost and confirm our date. Beth's job as president is to call the school district transportation services and schedule a bus. After the class leaves for recess, we 3 go to an available phone. Joey's call is quick. He writes down the information and goes outside to recess.

Beth's call is not as quick. The person who answers the phone listens to her request, hangs up. She calls back. Again, he hangs up. I make the 3rd call. The transportation supervisor is chagrined to realize the call is legitimate. "I'm sorry. I thought it was a student at home sick and having fun with me," he says. We hang up.

Beth makes the 4th call, schedules the bus, and heads outside to recess. It is now clear to me that a child's voice may not be taken seriously. In later years, students are taught to state their age and purpose at the beginning of their call.

After recess, Joey announces the cost, date, and time. Beth announces the bus schedule. The children clap. Emma, the class secretary, leads the class in writing a permission slip.

After a brief discussion of what the permission slip will say, the students dictate sentences. Included are the date and time, a request for permission, and the destination. Other important facts are bringing a sack lunch and money. Parents are invited to join us. After lots of board erasing, the class settles on the final sentences. Emma copies the information and takes it to the office to be typed and copies made. That night, the permission slips go home. A sample follows.

Dear Mom and Dad,

Our class is taking a trip to the zoo on April 10. I need $2.00 to get in.

I have to bring a sack lunch. The lunchroom will give us drinks.

I need 35 cents for my drink.

Please sign this permission slip so I can ride the school bus.

We will leave at 9:15 a.m. and return at 2:00 p.m.

If you want to come, please call Miss Carter.

Signature _____

Date_____

The following day, the class secretary collects the permission slips and takes them to the office. The treasurer collects $2.35 from each child and delivers the money to the lunchroom and the office. We are ready for our trip!

Note. Everyone returned their slips and money the next day. Independence and responsibility becomes part of being in charge.

Summary

A simple understanding of the concept of democracy starts at a young age. The idea of freedom to take action and the ability to stand up for what is right is not learned in an instant. It must be taught in schools.

This class learned that responsibility is needed to get things done. Their confidence will be necessary for what happens in the next article.

Democracy cannot succeed unless those who express
their choice are prepared to choose wisely.
The real safeguard of democracy, therefore, is education.
Franklin D. Roosevelt

1008.B PETITION TO THE SCHOOL BOARD

"Oh no," the students cry as they enter the classroom and hear the news. "Our all day field trip to the zoo is canceled by the School Board." After the 2nd graders settle down in their seats, a discussion begins.

What is a School Board? Why did they pass a rule that students have to eat lunch in the building? I explain that the lunchroom food orders need to be consistent. When students leave on a field trip, there is food left over, and money is wasted. The School Board does not want money wasted.

"What can we do?" they ask. One student says, "Let's just go anyway. We planned our trip first." He has a good point. Wanting them to learn the power of the people - or students - a petition is suggested.

After explaining how petitions work and how they are used, the class dictates their own version. Emma our class secretary writes it on the board. When everyone feels it says what is wanted, she copies it on a piece of paper large enough for everyone to sign. It is taped to the board.

Each child comes quietly to the front of the room and signs their first and last names. It is a big deal to stand up for their rights. The secretary places the petition in a large envelope and delivers it to the school office with a request that it be sent to the School Board chairman immediately as our trip is in a few days. Fortuitously, the School Board chairman has a child in our K-3 building, so the petition is sent home that day.

Two days later, a letter from the School Board arrives. In essence it says,

> March 14, 1968
> Dear Second Grade Class,
>
> Thank you for your petition. Since your class planned your field trip before we passed our new rule, we give you permission to go on your all-day field trip. The new rule will apply to all future field trips.
>
> The School Board of Education
> Endicott-Endwell, New York

students planned it and, as a class, fought for it. Democracy in action finds a foothold in this classroom of 2nd graders.

Summary

This class is in charge of many of the curriculum activities. They write a school play, adapt to a new concept of 'cluster grouping' of desks, and set up and perform science investigations. A new approach to teaching solidifies, *Let the students be in charge as much as possible.*

As confidence increases, students become effective and independent learners. Our nation's future, based on the input and participation of its citizens, is secure.

> *Never doubt that a small group of committed*
> *can change the world. Indeed it's the only thing that ever has.*
> Margaret Mead

1008.C SHOULD THE MAJORITY RULE?

Most people agree that a democratic approach means the majority rules. However, this article advances a new viewpoint.

Working together

An efficient team creates a plan to produce excellent results. A patched-together plan, based on who makes the final decisions, may end up in disagreements due to lack of support by certain individuals. A majority making the decisions does not guarantee success.

Community contest
This contest is conducted by a university. Three teams are competing to create the best plan for making a model of a community park. Although this seems unimportant to say now, 2 teams are Caucasian and one is Native American.

Challenge: Identify a plan for designing a 3-D Model for a Multipurpose City Park.

On the Monday morning of the contest, the teams are given a description of the challenge and told to take as long as they need to create the plan for building a model. Once all 3 groups complete their plans and a winner declared, that team will build the model of the park.

By Tuesday afternoon, 2 teams have checked in. The Native American team is still consulting among themselves. By Wednesday morning, the checked-in teams are commenting on the perceived inability of the 3rd team to come up with a plan. Late Wednesday afternoon, the last team appears with their plan in hand. A few puzzled and slightly disgruntled members of the other teams ask why they took so long. They explain.

"Your plans are designed based on the underlying belief that the majority must rule. Ideas that don't fit with the majority are set aside or ignored. With no protracted disagreements and discussions, your plans are finished sooner.

Our Native culture doesn't do that. First, we discuss each detail so every member contributes. Adjustments are made until a final plan emerges that is *thoroughly analyzed and to which everyone on the team agrees*."

With the individual as an important part of the whole, this approach indeed demonstrates 'true democracy.'

The Native American plan, based on its thorough analysis by a fully committed team, takes the prize. Not bound by 'majority rule,' all ideas are considered valid. Everyone agrees with and supports the final plan.

Summary

The answer to "Should the majority rule?" is often an automatic, 'Yes.' Yet the majority rule cancels the minority and means useful ideas may be lost. It becomes clear that 'inclusive collaboration' is more likely to succeed. To consider all ideas produces a strong and clear basis for the final outcome.

The process of such detailed collaboration leads to effective work in teams, families, and town hall meetings.
1001.E STUDENT COLLABORATION
1002.B ENRICH COLLABORATION - BUTTERFLIES

> *One man with courage is the majority.*
> Thomas Jefferson

1008.D WARS BEGIN WITH DISAGREEMENTS

A high school teacher asks for a lesson in her classroom that models 100% class participation. WWII is introduced with 2 open-ended questions. As a war is basically an enormous argument, each question relates to understanding arguments.

TEACHER "What *causes* people to get into arguments?"
First, students collaborate with a partner. After a few minutes, a class discussion follows.

STUDENT ANSWERS (shortened to its key point)

- Different points of view.
- An argumentative nature.
- Misunderstandings.
- Lack of compassion.
- Desire to be the winner.
- A demand to be right at all costs.
- Fear of being a victim.
- An incomplete picture of the situation.
- Unwillingness to find common ground.
- Inability to find a solution due to differing points of view.

These answers are from young adults involved in the lesson..

The second question identifies possible effects.
TEACHER "What are the *effects of* arguments?"
STUDENT ANSWERS
- Refusal to communicate.
- Shout without listening.
- Pointed teasing.
- Threats.
- Outrageous behaviors.
- Physical attacks.
- Personality attacks.
- Stubbornness.
- Unkindness such as mocking.
- Reminders of past mistakes.
- War.

As arguing is a personal experience these are tough questions to discuss. Therefore, the atmosphere is kept positive and upbeat. When a student points out the problems another student has with arguing, the behavior is squelched. "We're here to learn about a war, not start one!" Laughter defused the tension.

The homework assignment is to interview either a family member or a neighbor who fought in a war. Two questions are asked, "What caused the war? and "What were the effects of the war? Why?" The class is reminded that personal feelings are not to be included as the focus is on facts.

Summary
Their interviews are shared the following day. Their teacher now has a solid base for teaching WWII. With a supportive environment and a positive atmosphere, participation reaches 100%.

Note. Several high school teachers ask to see a demonstration of this open-ended question approach demonstrated in their classroom. One teacher points out that a student who never speaks contributed 3 times. Another teacher is impressed by his class's willingness to participate as teacher assistants.

Authentic learning is based on a supportive atmosphere that challenges the students' imagination and intelligence. This brings out the best in everyone.

> *The single biggest problem in communication*
> *is the illusion that it has taken place.*
> George Bernard Shaw

Story
During a summer class about Native Americans, a new type of discipline is taught to the teachers. As Native American tribes can be small (sometimes between 15 and 50 people) each tribal member is valuable. If an individual's behavior threatens the tribe's harmony, a unique form of discipline is applied.

First, the entire tribe sits down to form a circle around the troublesome person who is seated in the center. Next, the compliments begin. The individual's value to the life of the tribe is reviewed. This may go on for days until the problem is completely reversed - cancelled - not only in the wayward person's mind, but in the minds of the tribal members. The tribe has to 'save' their tribe by convincing everyone of this person's worth.

This method emphasizes the importance of praise and gratitude. Every child who feels valued, is happier and becomes a better learner. Recognize and emphasize the child's goodness and innate self-worth blossoms.

1008.E MANDAN RESEARCH

Primary research discovers new information. It includes original experiments, ways to build cars, rockets, buildings, and asking questions.

Secondary research collects information from a variety of sources - old letters and news articles, scientific interpretations of carvings on cave walls, and travel magazines about volcanoes and earthquake regions. Examining photos, diagrams, and charts, the secondary researcher takes notes and creates a report along with charts and interpretations.

The Mandan Indians

A 4th grade enrichment group votes to study the Mandan Indians. During a trip to the public library, and with a helpful librarian, they find a file drawer of material collected by previous adult researchers. Notes are taken as the information cannot be checked out. With their notes, a movie, and books, they have a treasure trove of research materials.

Research goes beyond the Mandan's daily life and settlements. Nearby mountains, the effects of seasons, and migration routes add interesting details.

To expand their classmates' study of the West, this small group prepares a presentation. The gym floor is measured to show the size of the Indians' house. (40 feet across) A small corner of the stage is built as a replica of a Mandan home furnished with student crafted items. Their classmates walk through a real life diorama. Mini-presentations describe the research details.

Enjoying their extensive research, the group votes to continue studying the Mandan culture for the 2nd semester. Visting the diorama, one mother notes, "My son never stops talking about the Mandan Indians." Perhaps he is a future researcher.

Summary
Well-written reference books take students beyond the textbook and class lectures to in-depth information. For a child, opening a book to a random page, seeing photos comparable to artwork, and finding little known facts is like finding the treasures of the world - hidden in a book.

> *Research is formalized curiosity. It is poking and*
> *prying with a purpose.*
> Zora Neale Hurston

1008.F YORKTOWN EXCHANGE GROUPS
After a friend presents the Battle of Yorktown to his club and after reading the first chapters of this book, a specific history lesson is requested to be included in this book. It is suggested that students study the key men at the surrender of Yorktown, the last battle of the Revolutionary War.

The 5 people are - Alexander Hamilton, British General Lord Cornwallis, Lieutenant Colonel Tarlton, General George Washington, and James Armistead, later renamed James Armistead Lafayette.

As a secondary research activity, 5 small groups investigate one person's role at the battle. Each child in a group becomes an Expert. Reassigned to an Exchange group, each student shares what's been learned. Together the class discovers what happened at the 1781 Surrender of Yorktown.

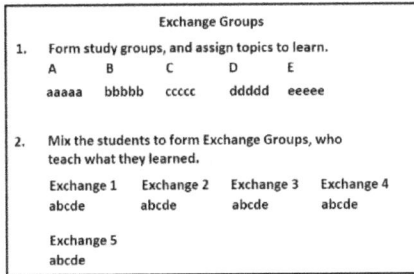

```
                    Exchange Groups
1.   Form study groups, and assign topics to learn.
     A       B       C       D       E
     aaaaa   bbbbb   ccccc   ddddd   eeeee

2.   Mix the students to form Exchange Groups, who
     teach what they learned.
     Exchange 1   Exchange 2   Exchange 3   Exchange 4
     abcde        abcde        abcde        abcde

     Exchange 5
     abcde
```

Note. As this is a decisive land victory in the Revolutionary War, students find information easily. Folklore says the British band played, "The World's Turned Upside Down" as the surrender takes place.

Summary

Through collaborative work, students gain a deeper meaning of the information. Lifelong skills develop as questions are investigated and details are explained. As they work, the teacher asks questions to guide their research.
Note. Years later as England battles to survive during WWII, their Prime Minister makes this statement.

We shall defend our island whatever the cost may be.
We shall fight on the beaches,
we shall fight on the landing grounds,
we shall fight in the fields
and in the streets, we shall fight in the hills,
we shall never surrender.
Winston Churchill

1008.G THE ROMAN EMPIRE

Every year, the Roman Empire in the social studies unit is a challenge for the 5th graders. Beginning with the legend of Romulus and Remus, the unit covers a series of emperors and wars - including Hannibal crossing the Alps with elephants in 218 B.C. to attack Rome. This is a strange scenario for 5th graders to grasp. As it's difficult to recall unfamiliar information, the final test grades are not the best.

One year, a new idea emerges - students will be 'assistant teachers.' Small groups will be responsible for teaching the class a few paragraphs in the textbook.

Background
During the 1st semester, students learn to collaborate in teams, present information to the class, and write test questions based on Benjamin Bloom's levels of thinking. Although a project of this size is planned - or even thought of - it seems the students have enough skills and confidence to take on the Roman Empire.

To begin
The teacher tells the students that they are in charge of learning and teaching the Roman Empire. The teacher will make sure they include the details of the final book test. Question. How do they want to present the information?

After a class discussion, they vote to have a play. The textbook pages are divided and paragraphs assigned to groups of 4 students. Ability levels are mixed as would be true in any business working group. Everyone is to work together to support their team.

Criteria
Each student is responsible for acting out information with their group. The mini-script for the group's play includes original research. Each student also writes 3 questions for the class to answer, and scores the answers. The final step is to explain the reason for the correct answers. This approach demands high levels of thinking.

Adding original facts found through research, the Roman Empire becomes more interesting and easily remembered. Each group practices their quizzes for accuracy. Everyone has to pass the quizzes as well as the final test.

Props are not allowed. If they need a fig tree, it is described, "Oh, look a fig tree! Look at the shiny small leaves, and the green fruit." No storing of props, no exceptions.

The class has 2 weeks to prepare for the play, and 2 days to present it. With all the activity in the room, students often pause to watch others. Discipline is barely needed as their final test grades are based on teamwork. Plus, they like being independent.

The final plays are amazing. Students, who seldom participate, boldly step to the front of the room and deliver their lines - memorized or with note cards. Mini-quizzes are given, checked, returned, and explained. 100% class participation is the foundation for success.

The following Monday, we begin our review for the unit test. Asking for a volunteer to tell about the Roman Empire, a shy youngster waves his hand. He begins, "Rome starts with a legend about the twins Romulus and Remus. They are left to die, but are raised by a she wolf." He pauses briefly with a confident look that says he wants to continue.

Hands fly into the air for the next turn. I shake my head. For the first time ever, this quiet child wants to speak. The class listens enthralled as he regales us with the details he's learned from his classmates. We are spellbound. When he finishes, the class spontaneously applauds and cheers. His face lights up. Admired by his peers, this once quiet, shy boy emerges as a happy and confident student.

The next day is the exam. Their quiz questions and the textbook questions are combined. However, one student is at a huge disadvantage, Taffy is not a strong reader. A new approach is tried.
1003.E A TEST READ IN MONOTONE

The Roman Empire grades are terrific. Averages go up. The class is thrilled. Me, too! Their dedicated efforts also contribute to a huge improvement in their national test scores.

The ITBS test, given nationwide at the end of the school year, expects students to improve one grade level. This year is different. The students know how questions are constructed and how to identify correct answers. Confident, they take on the big test challenge.

Note. After one part of the test, a high achiever hurries up to say, "There was one question that I had no idea what the answer was. I figured it out by picking the one based on what I knew about questions and answers." Her ability to 'figure out' an answer to a hard question impacts her score tremendously.

The class ITBS scores are phenomenal. The Assistant Superintendent visits to congratulate them. The class shows - including Taffy - almost 2 years growth. What happened? The students, able to analyze the thinking and implications behind test questions, learned to think like the adults who wrote the test.

Summary
The next teaching assignment is to teach the elementary school district enrichment classes - for 7 years. This new method of teaching continues

with small groups. Students become assistant teachers by researching their topic and learning how to write questions. Each child increases in their abilities and confidence.

Years later, this approach impacts my tutoring business. Continuing to teach children to analyze information, ask questions, and identify implications, confidence soon replaces self-doubt. Intelligence and self-worth improves as the child plays a larger role in learning. Grades go up. The tutoring builds a foundation for life.

Individual commitment to a group effort -
that is what makes a team work,
a company work, a society work, a civilization work.
Vince Lombardi

1008.H MARKET PLACE DAY

"Miss White's 1st grade is entering the 5th Grade Market Place. Welcome!" A giant metal gong reverberates as the children hurry to the selling booths to buy their favorite item.

Two classes of 5th graders are managing the marketplace. They handle making change and wrapping purchases in tissue paper. The gong sounds again. "Mrs. Steitzer's 3rd grade class is now leaving. Thank you for coming."

Background
The Fifth Grade Marketplace Day is the culmination of studying marketplaces around the world. The money earned pays for an all-day field trip to the Amana Colonies, an independent cooperative community half an hour south of the school.

To begin, the students identify items to sell, make samples, then take them to the other classrooms. The younger students vote for their favorites. Based on the items with the most votes, the class decides how many should be made. The yearly favorite is a silk flower corsage for Mother's Day.

Note. Their original research pays off as almost all the items are sold.

Each day, the class completes their schoolwork in record time, so they have craft-making time at the end of the day. (Classes are self-contained.) As the children support each other in completing their classwork, seldom did anyone have homework.

Students bring materials purchased at home. Teams create the items similar to an assembly line, then check them for quality control. Shy children blossom as they learn to be comfortable and successful in working with their classmates. As Market Place Day approaches, bags and tissue paper are brought from home to package the sold items.

The class treasurer calls to rent a city bus. The class secretary designs and keeps track of the permission slips. The class president and vice president contact the Amanas to set up a tour. We discuss proper manners for visiting the restaurant and getting off and on the bus. Gratitude for adults' help is emphasized as appreciation goes a long way toward being treated well.
1011.I WILLINGNESS TO BE FAIR

Visiting the Amanas, the students go in and out of the blacksmith's barn, people's homes, and the communal kitchen. It is a day of acting as, and being treated as, adults. The real life test is being independent and confident, solving problems, and caring for and about each other. They pass. During our trip, one waitress notes that this is the best group of students the waitresses have ever seen.

Summary
This is the same class that taught each other the Roman Empire. Based

on this marketplace activity, the 5th graders learn how to start a business based on original research.

Our 2nd semester is one student-centered activity after another with the students teaching the curriculum and contributing to test questions. Mutual respect is an underlying theme as everyone is needed. It is quite a class. I am privileged to know them. Authentic learning gives the responsibility and learning techniques to the students.

America's future will be determined
by the home and the school.
The child becomes largely what he is taught,
hence we must watch what we teach, and how we live.
Jane Addams

1008.I THE ONE ROOM SCHOOL HOUSE
History
Founded in Prussia in the 1700's, the concept of the one-room schoolhouse quickly spread around the world to include Canada, New Zealand, and Ireland. Started in the United States in the 1800's, rural children from kindergarten through 8th grade attend these schools. A few U.S. Presidents including John Adams and Lyndon Johnson are students of the one room schoolhouse.

Parents build the schools out of local materials ranging from wood to thick sod dug from the prairie grasses. A single wood stove provides heat. The teacher's slate board is painted black, while the students have individual slates for math and writing practice.

The academic subjects - the 3 R's reading, writing and 'rithmetic - are taught to all ages. With one room containing several grade levels, the young students are helped by the older students which prepares them to be future teachers.

Due to low salaries, the teacher stays in the students' homes for a month at a time getting to know the students and their families. A Kentuckian wrote of his education in the 1940's.

> "The teachers that taught in the one room rural schools are special people. During the winter months, they get to the school early to start a fire in the potbelly stove, so the building is warm when the students arrive. On many occasions, they prepare a hot, noon meal on top of the stove usually consisting of soup or a stew of some kind. They take care of their students like a mother hen cares for her newly hatched chicks, always looking out for their health and welfare."

Summary
As the nation's population grows, the schools change. Children are divided by age for instruction. The spiral curriculum is based on introducing concepts one year then repeating and reviewing them the following years.

With today's technology, students rarely teach each other, the computer does the teaching. And yet, when students collaborate, information is better understood and is remembered longer.
1001.A SAVE THE MUSIC SUBSTITUTE

The greatness of America lies not in being more enlightened than any
other nation, but rather in her ability
to repair her faults.
Alexis de Tocqueville

1008.J FAMOUS PEOPLE AND FASCINATING FACTS
"Which revolutionary war hero refused to ride a horse?" Puzzled looks. "His initials are S.A." "Samuel Adams!" comes the answer.

Young students need more than short descriptions of events, people, and time periods unrelated to their world. Fascinating information enriches and solidifies history into their long term memory.

Story
Revolutionary leaders Sam Adams and John Hancock are staying in the Hancock-Clark House in Lexington when word comes that the enemy British soldiers, the Redcoats, are headed their way. Colonists, even from neighboring states, fill the village square as a show of force.

Adams and Hancock jump into a horse-drawn wagon and ride away from the approaching army. Suddenly, Adams realizes he's left a small trunk at the inn. Inside is a list of the names of the revolutionaries. If the British finds the trunk, they'll have proof of those fighting against King George III of England. The list means a hanging of the rebels.

Unhitching the horse, Hancock rides back to the inn, runs inside between bullets, and grabs the trunk. Jumping back on the horse, he rides to join Adams, and they make their escape. The wagon, although slower, is necessary. Adams does not like riding horses.

Note. When signing the Declaration of Independence, John Hancock signs his name first. While writing his signature in large letters, legend says he announces, "There! I guess King George will be able to read that without his spectacles!"

Summary
History becomes real when students choose a person or event to investigate, and share their facts with the class. Keeping track of their references proves the validity of the research.

Research
In the world of research, solid conjectures, good guesses, and hypotheses are accepted as true *even if original research is not possible.* Well-trained researchers *figure out* the accuracy of a fact based on their previous research.

Since these historical conjectures, although plausible, have *not been proven* to be correct, our world is but a *grand interpretation* by those who speak for it. Researchers write history.

> *History will be kind to me for I intend to write it.*
> Winston Churchill

1008.K PACKING A CONESTOGA WAGON

For these 2 class sessions, decision making is combined with packing a Conestoga wagon. The students had studied the dangers of crossing the Great American Desert and the Rocky Mountains to reach Oregon. Now the 5th graders are to decide the best item for them to bring on the long trip West.

The limitations of packing a Conestoga wagon become real as students make their decision using these 4 steps.
- Ask a key question that defines the decision.
- Identify optional answers or solutions.
- Ask criteria/probing questions to identify the best solution.
- State logical reasons for the final decision.

Day 1

The Scenario

A family of 2 parents and 2 children arrive at the Mississippi River with everything they own. Their plan is to travel to Oregon with a train of 100 wagons. Starting in May, they will have time to cross the Rocky Mountains before snow makes travel impossible. The cost to move is $1,000, which is around $35,000 today.

Planning and packing a Conestoga wagon takes time as efficiency is needed to keep the wagon upright. Supplies are needed for 2 months travel and to set up a homestead in Oregon. Looking over their personal belongings, the children are now limited to one item each. (Mind you, this specific scenario supports the decision making activity.)

Each 5th grader plays the role of a child in deciding a single item. The goal is written on the board, *Use decision making to choose one item to take to Oregon.*

*Decision Making

Question. "What is the *best* item for me (the child) to bring to Oregon in the Conestoga wagon? (All crucial details are included in the question.)

*List of items

A small rifle, doll, knitting needles and yarn, a button collection, a set of 3 knives, a box of Nature items, an arrowhead collection, a recipe book, a doll and doll clothes, a jump rope, marbles, books, and a fiddle. Each student chooses 5 items and lists them on a piece of paper.

*Criteria

Based on traveling in the wagon and a new life in Oregon, students identify 5 probing questions. These questions help them to think about each item and narrow the list down to 1.

How to write a criteria question

'Yes' must mean the same thing each time a question is answered. A *'positive yes'* means the item is a good choice. Compare these 2 'yes' answers.

'Is this item light enough for the Conestoga wagon?' A 'yes' means the item is light and *is a good choice.*

'Is this item too heavy for the Conestoga wagon?'

A 'yes' now means the item is too heavy and *is not a good choice.*

The following criteria fit the *'positive yes'* answer. The students discuss what is meant by each question - which is in italics.

Probing Questions
Q1. Is it small in size? *The item takes little space in the wagon.*
Q2. Is it light in weight? *By being light more weight is allowed for supplies.*
Q3. Is it useful at our new home? *In Oregon, we'll be glad we have it to help us get started in a faraway place.*
Q4. Is it hard to replace? *It must have a high value as getting a new one is next to impossible.*
Q5. Can anyone in the family use it? *We want others to be able to use the item.*

Note. These questions take time to write.
Note. An odd number of items means only one item will have the points needed to be chosen. With an even number, there may be a tie.

Charts are handed out. Each child lists his/her 5 choices
from A to E. (Or their written list is labeled A to E).
Q1 - Q5 matches the questions on the board.

*Procedure
Ask question 'Q1.' Apply it to each item… A-E.
Decide 'yes' or 'no' for each question, and write the letter 'Y' or 'N' next to the item on the chart.

Chart for Packing the Conestoga Wagon							
Item	Q1	Q2	Q3	Q4	Q5	YES	NO
A							
B							
C							
D							
E							

Summary for Day 1

The activity took an hour. The classroom teacher provided more time for the students to ask their questions and answer 'yes/no.' The totals of 'yes' and 'no' were written to the right. The next day, we will finish the final steps.

Day 2

Looking over the charts the next day, it was clear that the students had convinced their teacher to let them make changes. The new questions for # 3 and #4 are now,

Is this your favorite item?

Will you be sad if you leave it behind?

Their totals now include feelings rather than practicality. We discuss whether our feelings will help us travel West or start a homestead in Oregon. We have a good laugh. The original questions are reinstated and charts updated.

Chart A

Chart for Packing the Conestoga Wagon							
Item	Q1	Q2	Q3	Q4	Q5	YES	NO
A rifle	N	N	Y	N	Y	2	3
B knife	Y	Y	Y	N	Y	4	1
C arrow-heads	Y	Y	N	N	N	2	3
D marbles	Y	Y	N	N	Y	3	2
E fiddle	N	N	N	Y	N	1	4

The highest total of yeses for the knife made it the final choice. To identify the *reasons* it is best, we refer to the criteria questions. According to this child's chart,

"The best item to bring is the knife set because it is small in size, lightweight, and will be useful at our new home, and others can use it.

Chart B

	Chart for Packing the Conestoga Wagon						
Item	Q1	Q2	Q3	Q4	Q5	YES	NO
A doll	N	N	N	Y	N	1	4
B yarn	N	Y	Y	N	Y	3	2
C jump rope	Y	Y	N	N	Y	3	2
D 2 books	N	N	N	Y	Y	2	3
E recipe box	Y	N	Y	Y	Y	4	1

"The best item to bring is the recipe box because it is small in size, lightweight, hard to replace, and it can be used by others."

Summary
Travel on the Oregon Trail begins in 1843. Smart planning plus sensible decisions makes the difference between arriving in California or dying in the snows of the Rocky Mountains. With effective decision making skills, families have a better chance of reaching Oregon.

For the 5th grade students, decision making becomes a lifetime skill.

History
On May 10, 1869 "the Last Spike' - ahead of time and under budget - is driven into the railroad tracks connecting the East and West coasts of the United States. As trains are more efficient, the Conestoga wagons are soon no more. The United States is on its way to becoming a global power.

Note. The wagons are made in Conestoga Valley in Lancaster County in Pennsylvania.
Note. There are excellent film shorts on the Internet about the growth of USA railroads.

Every day is a journey, and the journey itself is home.
Matsuo Basho

Note. If the sole purpose is to introduce decision making, the fairy tale of Cinderella is used. Her key question is, "What is the best way to go to the ball?" This decision making activity is on the Internet. Search for: *Cinderella decides how to go to the ball.*   Lovinteachin's Blog

CHAPTER 8 IN CONCLUSION
A CULTURE'S FOUNDATION. SOCIAL STUDIES AND HISTORY

Faced with dates and facts, students memorize them only to forget them after the test. Alternative methods of study improve long term memory.

From small groups of 'experts' involved in secondary research to a real life market place to a play about the Roman Empire, an integrated approach with a high level of participation brings history into the students' lives. History becomes fascinating facts to tell their future children.

Story
A college history professor focuses his lectures on the economic and societal effects resulting from The Great War and World War II. Listening to him regale the details of daily life is like sitting at the feet of a family elder telling the history of our country. Historical facts combines with personal knowledge of the time period, to make the course memorable.

Fascinating details of a time, place, and people added to class lectures keeps children 100% interested.

There are no extraordinary men…
just extraordinary circumstances
that ordinary men are forced to deal with.
William Halsey

PART I
Enrichment Ideas

Chapter 9 Classroom Management

Chapter 10 Classroom Setting

Chapter 11 A Plethora of Ideas

Chapter 12 #realstorieshappen

Index
Sources
Miss Trudi's Bio
A Student's Perspective

Chapter 9
Classroom Management

Establish an organization for basics, then act

Topics
A. Clean Classroom   B. Hall Walking   C. ABCD's of Kindness
D. Assign Numbers   E. Study Teams   F. Spontaneity

Introduction
Harmony happens when classroom procedures are orchestrated in a simple manner. As a management process is analyzed then implemented, every day procedures become familiar to the students.

With clear expectations, children are orderly, calm,, self-disciplined, and self-assured. This allows more time for lessons, assignments, and enjoying the day.

With participatory approaches, such as proper hall behavior and handing out worksheets, students soon realize that working together supports everyone. Time is saved and kindness abounds. In turn, organizational skills transfer to managing their own lives easily and effectively. Supporting each other to meet group goals, children grow and blossom.

The achievement of an organization is the result
of the combined efforts of each individual.
Vince Lombardi

1009.A ONE MINUTE TO A CLEAN CLASSROOM
I absolutely love how well this activity brought the children together with a common goal. From a clean classroom to enhanced self-esteem to reading a clock's second hand, and learning how to clean, there are benefits galore! Here is how the 'event' unfolds.

Time to Beautify the Classroom

The children sit tall at their desks, hands folded, eyes fastened on the clock. As the second hand moves toward the 12, the teacher counts out loud, "5, 4, 3, 2, 1…Go!" Students rush to their pre-arranged work assignment. Boards are wiped clean. Pencil sharpeners are emptied. Papers on the floor are picked up and put in the wastebasket which is placed by the door for the custodian. Students who finish early call out, "Who needs me?" and run to assist. If the holler, "Help!" is heard, a classmate speeds over to provide assistance.

During the minute's last five seconds, the countdown reverses, "5..4..3..2..1!" Students run to their desks, slide into their seats, and fold their hands ready to bask in well-deserved admiration. Gazing around the room, I say appreciatively, "Look how shiny the boards are! The floor looks so neat." Students join in to compliment the good work - even the emptied pencil sharpeners are noticed! Those who helped another child are thanked. We're ready for tomorrow - a new day in our orderly and sparkling clean classroom.

Set up
At the end of the first week of school, the plan is discussed and established. After describing the joy of having a clean classroom - its beauty and organization – the question comes, "In what ways can we clean and organize our classroom at the end of the day?" Writing their ideas on the board, two person jobs are labeled '2.'

A number tag is drawn from the 'taking turns' jar. The first child writes their number by a job. Continuing to draw numbers, the students choose their tasks.

Note. By listing more tasks than students, the last child has a choice.

The jobs are then listed on a large sheet of cardboard. Clothespins with student numbers are clipped next to their job. Each week, the clothespins are moved in the same direction for one space. Children are allowed to trade for the week. Short weeks are added to the coming week.

Custodians appreciate our clean classroom. They have more time to scrub the floor and dust cupboards. The teacher has more time to grade papers and write lesson plans - or leave on time. :) A science lesson contributes to clean desk tops.

1007.F MEASURE BUBBLES

Summary
Being responsible together contributes to positive attitudes among the students. A child, happy and proud of their contributions in class, looks forward to the next school day. Over time, the children become more orderly, even reminding each other to pick up a scrap of paper or straighten a book.

When a visiting adult compliments the class on their calm and orderly atmosphere, the children beam happily. If it's a young class, the children receive an M&M. (see 1009.D.)

If you want to build a ship, don't drum up people
to collect wood and don't assign them tasks and work,
but rather teach them to long for the endless immensity of the sea.
Antoine de Saint-Exupery

Learning to 'love and yearn for' a clean classroom, children cheerfully keep it that way all day long.

1009.B HALL WALKING AND REWARDS
Our school has long hallways. When the line of students stretches down the hall, the teacher faces 3 choices: walk near the middle, the front, or

the back. The bottom line? Keep an eye on the class. Over the years, techniques develop to stay alert to the students.

1. Class Line Leader. Before the class leaves the room, the line leader is told where to stop. When the last child steps out of the room, the door is locked, and the teacher catches up to the line leader. Directed to the next stopping point, the class again follows. This start and stop method makes it easy to watch over the children.

2. Signals. Eventually, signals guide the line leader. At the stopping point, the leader turns around to check the teacher's hand signal to go further down the hall or turn the corner. The teacher stays at the back and watches the line. The children enjoy the freedom of moving forward on their own.

3. More Signals. A hand held high means 'stop' to the line leader and brings the class to a gentle halt - like dominos bumping, but not falling. A wave of the hand moves the leader forward. Every child watches and learns where to stop and when to go. Every child is ready to be a line leader.

M&M rewards
If an adult walks by and compliments the 1st graders 'quiet hall' behavior, one finger is help up. The youngsters grin happily as it means they receive an M&M. Another adult compliment at the water fountain? Another M&M.

When we return to the classroom, the child in charge of the M&Ms stands by the door with an open wooden box filled with the colorful chocolates. As the children file into the room, they choose one. Watching the children carefully decide which color M&M to take makes me smile as the inside is always chocolate.

Although a simple reward, the M&M encourages proper group behavior. Of special importance is that an adult, other than the teacher, gives the compliment.

Group walk
The older students are allowed to walk in small groups and whisper. However, if a classroom teacher complains about the noise as they go by, they walk in a silent line the next day. During the entire year, there is never a silent line. The principal notes that this class is the only one that walks so quietly. It appears that older children like to be treated as adults.

Summary
Trusting the students' desire for independence and giving the class opportunities for self-discipline, creates confident, calm children who understandingly follow the rules.

> *Civilization is a method of living, an attitude*
> *of equal respect for all men.*
> Jane Adams

1009.C ABCD'S OF KINDNESS
It's pure serendipity. A 4th grader goes out of her way to help another classmate. During the 'end of the day' class discussion, her kindness is mentioned. Suddenly, a military term comes to thought. "That's going Above and Beyond the Call of Duty." Writing the term on the board, it's observed that the student's faces are blank.

Explaining how the term is used in the military, someone notices that the first letters are ABCD. An idea is born and a question asked. "At the end of the day, shall we share when someone performs an ABCD kindness?" "Yes!" comes the resounding chorus. The 4th graders are off and running with excitement.

First, they identify a list of kindnesses. From opening a door to letting someone go first at the water fountain to carrying someone's lunch tray, their list grows. Someone suggests that points be given for being kind. Picking up a dropped pencil is 5 points while letting someone cut in line is 10. A student offers to design numbered circles at home on her computer. My job is making the cardboard copies. Taking the circles home, the children decorate them, cut them out, and bring them back for laminating.

Once we have our stack of circles - they are beautiful! - being kind becomes an art. At the end of the day, the class identifies acts of kindness, and the numbered circles are handed out. Plastic baggies keep them safe.

Soon, the motive behind the act becomes as important as the kindness itself. Doing something just for points is not acceptable. To my surprise, students give them to each other. The idea of kindness spreads. Visiting parents mention their child's kindnesses at home.

As the end of the year nears, the question arises, "What can we do with our points?" An auction is decided. Cleaned out closets and teacher purchases at the local thrift shop provide auction items. The day arrives. The rule is 3 bids per item. It is also explained, "Items might run out." The children's answer? "No problem."

As we start the auction, it's noticed that the quietest boy has no ABCD circles. His classmates explain that each time he earns a circle, he passes it to someone else. One student makes a suggestion - and it is agreed upon by all - he is to be first to choose from the auction items. The teacher is grateful for the class's ultimate kindness. With a delighted smile, he makes his choice, and the auction begins. They bid, trade items, and change their minds. It is a wonderful time.

Summary
This activity happens in the second half of the school year after the first
semester teacher leaves for maternity leave. The children's caring about
each other through this unique activity softens the missing of a beloved
teacher. Children love to love, be loved and to be kind.

> *The best portion of a good man's life is his little*
> *nameless, unremembered acts of kindness and love.*
> William Wordsworth

1009.D FIRST, ASSIGN US NUMBERS

Assigning the students numbers proves a unique way to keep track of
papers and whose turn it is for a classroom activity. An Answer Poem
guarantees success.

How to
At the end of the first week, the alphabetized class list is numbered
starting with 101. Those who join the class later have their names
inserted alphabetically with a 'b' after their number. For instance, 117
for Hickson is followed by the new student's number 117b for Johnson.

With numbers written under their names, assignments are quickly put in
alphabetical order which makes grades easy to record. For privacy on test
papers, only the numbers are used. When drawings, poetry, or holiday
pictures are hung in the hallway, the student's number is written on the
back.

Answering questions
To be sure all children have a chance to answer questions, cardboard tags
are numbered with the children's numbers and dropped into a jar. When
a question is asked, a tag is taken out and that child gives the answer.
Once pulled out, the tag goes into a different jar.

What if the child doesn't know the answer? This unique procedure guarantees a student's success.
1001.G AN ANSWER POEM

Mailboxes
* Flyers from the principal's office and PTA announcements plus assignments make a large stack. How to ensure every child takes the right papers home? Classroom mailboxes.

Cardboard cartons (used to transport heavy bottles) are covered in contact paper. Student numbers are written above the openings. This makes it quick and easy to pop in the papers. Papers are handed out as the students' load their backpacks to go home.

*Absent students often end up behind in assignments. At the beginning of the year, students identify someone to take their papers and books home to them. Typically, it is a brother or sister. Another child, who rides the same bus, passes the materials to the sibling. Sometimes a parent picks up the assignments. Returning to school, the child is ready to participate. Get well cards from the class are included.

Summary
Although numbers are helpful for organization, students write their names on their papers, too. Kinder and more personal, a signature is also required as a lifelong skill. (see Cursive book: *Swoops, Loops, and Curls - From Print to Cursive* Trudi Carter 2024)

Note. Allowing children or adults to sort graded assignments into the mailboxes is not a good idea. Student grades are no longer private. Therefore, the graded papers are sorted at noon by the teacher and the school announcement papers are put on top. This ensures the children's privacy.

Never be in a hurry, do everything quietly and in a calm spirit.
Do not lose your inner peace for anything whatsoever,
even if your whole world seems upset.
Francis de Sales

1009.E IDENTIFY STUDY TEAMS

Yes, the student is expected to function independently. Indeed, that's a key purpose of this book. Yet in a team, collaboration develops the ability to think by talking out loud. A study team is a valuable tool for learning and understanding.

Set up
At first, students chose their own partner. Not surprisingly problems arise. Who knew that friendships divert attention? Or, if one student already understands the information, the other student doesn't contribute. Collaboration goes more smoothly when the study teams are teacher assigned - one for math, one for reading and writing.

The key is basing the team on ability level. Quick thinkers spark and challenge each other; deliberate thinkers have more time to sort ideas. Independent work comes later as success replaces fear of failure. The 2 boys in lesson 1005.F broke through their previous failures by meeting a new challenge together.

Deliberate
What makes a child a slow worker? It may not be lack of ability. A teacher is concerned about Howard's lack of completed assignments. His mother worries about poor grades. Howard is asked, "Why are you so slow at writing?" His answer is a surprise.

"Do you know how long it takes to decide exactly which word fits best in a sentence and makes the most sense? It takes time to do a good job." Howard's explanation reveals that he is a *deliberate thinker*. Allowed to finish writing assignments at home, his grades improve.

*Confidence
As the year progresses, study teams gain confidence. Eventually, the deliberate worker completes his assignment alone. High achieving students work for their personal best, Class participation increases. The best part? The study team is always there to help analyze and figure out the assignment.

Note. A long period of collaboration time is wearying. At some point the sharing stops, and the teacher continues the lesson. When class enthusiasm indicates success is happening, set a time frame, "We have one more minute for discussion," or set a simple goal. "When everyone has written a sentence, put your pencil down, and we'll continue." The teacher is the guide.

Summary
Collaboration is a chief key for learning - it lowers stress, improves academic understanding, and pops with new ideas. Whether it's reading a textbook page, 'quick checking' an answer, or completing an assignment, a team partner provides support. Praising the students' teamwork techniques, keeps them focused on proper collaboration. (see Chapter 1) The best part for the students? They are doing the learning and thinking.

Alone we do so little; together we can do so much.
Helen Keller

1009.F SPONTANEITY
Creative ideas often happen quite suddenly and lend interest to the school work.

*Number Sentences
Reviewing addition facts in math class, students are asked to think of 'many ways' to write a number sentence whose answer is 9.
At first, the class focuses on addition. $4+5 = 9$ $1+1+1+1+5 = 9$
A child asks to use subtraction. $12-3 = 9$ $15-5-1 = 9$
Then someone combines the two processes. $10 - 4 + 3 = 9$

Excited by this example, the math teams go wild with new number sentences. This math lesson goes way beyond practicing addition facts.

Note. Recording student ideas on the board encourages 'the domino effect.'

*Math rule
To emphasize analysis in solving a math problem, a very long number sentence is written on the board. $(5x5) + (4+1) - (18+6) x0 = 9$
The question is, "Will the answer be 9? Yes or no."

At first, students start to do the math. Someone spots multiplying by zero and says, "The answer is not 9." He's asked not to tell the class how he figured it out so fast. The group continues working. More hands go up. "The answer is not 9." Soon the whole class realizes that multiplying by '0' means the answer is '0' not 9.

*Force Fit
Reviewing facts about the American Revolution, the lesson becomes 'ask a question, give an answer.' The alphabet, written in cursive above the chalkboard, triggers a new idea.

It is suggested, "Let's put together an alphabet book about the American Revolution." Student attention immediately increases to 100%.

Students are assigned sets of letters to combine with historical facts. Our results are delightful. A simple booklet is made. The test scores are great

American Revolution... 1765 – 1783
Bunker Hill ...Outside Boston. Under siege on June 17, 1775.
Colonials ...start a revolt on April 19, 1775.
Dawes, William ...rides to warn the colonists 900 Redcoats are coming on April 18, 1775
England ..Where the Redcoats come from.

A force fit combines ideas not usually found together. Using the alphabet letters, teams pore over the social studies book for facts. Sharing their results becomes a test review

Summary

Spontaneity encourages camaraderie, reduces stress, and increases understanding. New ideas pop. Long term memory happens. Test grades go up. Creative ideas keep schoolwork interesting.

> *A creative man is motived by a desire to achieve,*
> *not by the desire to beat others.*
> Ayn Rand

CHAPTER 9 IN CONCLUSION
CLASSROOM MANAGEMENT

Basic management procedures begin with clearly defined goals that establish proper patterns for student behavior. The substitute in Chapter 1 applied the essence of organization to create a successful lesson. When students work in 'similar ability' study teams, they learn how to support and challenge each other with new ideas. Teaching children to take care of their classroom leads to self-discipline. Responsibility and freedom develop over time.

Studying ants' management systems
 A class study of 'ant organization' and their behaviors seems to prove they are similar to the lives of people. However, when it's discovered that *ants build bridges with their bodies to allow other ants to race quickly across to their destination,* the class decided the ants .were mimicking our bridges
1007.I ANTS AND ORIGINAL RESEARCH

However, editor Bruce mentions that during the Revolutionary War, a 'body bridge' is used for Alexander Hamilton to climb to the top of the 10th parapet of a fort at the Battle of Yorktown. We are more like ants than we know.

Independent thinkers must never be full time sheep. Instead, they originate new ideas, positively impact society, and, in the long run, improve our world.

> *I am not afraid of an army of lions led by a sheep.*
> *I am afraid of an army of sheep led by a lion.*
> Alexander the Great

Chapter 10
Classroom Setting and Atmosphere

Let the surroundings support the work

Topics
Part I. A. Art   B. Music   C. Quotations   D. Fragrance
E. Room Designs … **Part II.**   F. Principal's Impact
G. Silent Signals   H. Gratitude and Praise   I. Fairness
J. Honesty   K. Trust   L. Mood

Introduction
Classroom Setting
Imagine entering a classroom with soft but bright lights and a fiscus tree lending a touch of greenery. The music of Beethoven plays, and beautiful artwork is on the walls. The desks are arranged for privacy and space. Bookshelves hold neatly arranged and easily accessible materials.

An interest table offers regalia and reading materials linked to the subjects being studied. Everything gleams thanks to the class clean-up activity the previous day. Inside the students' desks, orderliness means belongings are easy to find. Being in this classroom is a delight.

The Atmosphere
This did not happen on our 'first day'! Although the room is bleak, the children's supportive behavior creates an upbeat mood. With their loving care and a teacher guided by humility, an atmosphere of kindness and cooperation creates a delightful place for learning.

PART I
SETTING

1010.A ART IMPACTS INTELLIGENCE

Yes! is the emphatic answer to the question, 'Should art be in the classroom?'

Artwork reflects orderliness, harmony, joy, and an intensity of colors. As art impacts how students think and feel, choose classical art - a proven positive influence on sentiments and intelligence. When a student's attention wanders off the classwork to the walls, the artwork recalls class discussions of the art critics' evaluations. The child may glance away from the lesson at hand, but thinking is taking place.

Well-known art includes art critics' reviews. Discussing different critics' viewpoints, students gain new ways to reason. This unique form of analysis, with its new vocabulary and phrases, translates into a better learner.

Consider this painting by Frederic Edwin Church titled "Niagara From the American Side." The Niagara River comes from Canada. Its 3 waterfalls are usually viewed from a park in New York State. The Internet has several videos that are worth sharing with your class.

"Niagara Falls from the American Side"
Frederic Edwin Church   1857
40 inches by 90 inches

Hanging at the National Gallery of Art in Washington D.C.,
a nearby art critic's message says,

"Church's majestic 1857 canvas reveals the vista from the
Canadian shore. Based on oil and pencil sketches he made
during several visits to the site in 1856, he is the first to render
the spectacle on such a grand scale, with such fine detail,
naturalism, and immediacy.

Mr. Church heightens the illusion of reality by selecting a non-
traditional format of canvas with a width twice as wide as its
height to convey the panoramic expanse of the scene. He
eliminates any suggestion of a foreground allowing the viewer to
experience the scene as if precariously positioned on the brink of
the falls. As one writer enthusiastically notes, "This is Niagara,
with the roar left out!"

The aim of art is to represent not the outward
appearance of things, but their inward significance.
Aristotle

The Classics (Mona Lisa)
An elementary art teacher posts 15 examples of well-known artwork
above the white board. At the beginning of each class, the students recite
the title of each picture and its artist. The teacher then thoroughly
analyzes one painting. Developing an ability to understand and evaluate
art, student art work improves.

Portraits (George Washington)
Black and white photos of famous Americans related to the social studies curriculum are posted around a 2nd grade classroom. During a lesson, the information is connected to the person's picture. This makes the facts more relevant and memorable.

Summary
By discussing well-known artwork, even for a brief on-your-way-out-the-door -moment, the children's ability to analyze and evaluate expands. The art critics' viewpoints add original insight and vocabulary. Youngsters become thoughtful as they define and understand the artist's thinking behind the art. Enjoying art in the classroom uplifts and spurs students to success. Yes! Art must be in the classroom.

Every artist dips his brush in his own soul,
and paints his own nature into his pictures.
Henry Ward Beecher

1010.B CLASSICAL MUSIC AND SONG
An Accelerated Learning course emphasizes playing classical

music while students study. According to the research explained by Libyan Cassone, classical music - with its mathematical harmony and rhythm - impacts long term memory. I decide to try it.

As the 5th graders review their notes for a social studies test, Bach's prelude plays softly. "Will the test scores improve?" The next day, the tests are handed out. The students sit quietly. Asking why no one is taking the test, a student answers, "I can't remember a thing without the music playing." Bach's music is turned on.

Although music locks a connection to the information, it appears that, without the music playing, long term memory disappears. The research does not mention this. Hmm. If the students hear a Bach prelude in the future, will they recall their social studies facts?

After this experience, classical music fills the room at the beginning and end of the school day as the children enter and leave the room. An unexpected bonus? With music playing, students talk more quietly.

For some students, to study with music playing is a delight. For others, it's a distraction. For a few, it's pure anguish. Why the difference? It's their learning styles. If a student learns best by listening, then music supports study time. For other types of learners, music distracts to different degrees. This does not referring to classical music.
1011.H HOW LEARNING HAPPENS - AVK

Song
Singing is not typically found in our 4th grade classroom. However, during the Revolutionary War unit, a childhood music class is remembered as singing Yankee Doodle. A favorite song of the rebellious colonists, the music teacher came to our room and played it on a lap harp, and the class sang lustily.

Handing out the words, I sing the first verse.. The class is invited to join in. As we sing lustily, a knock on the door brings a message from the next door teacher. "We are taking a test. The singing is loud." Miss Brown. I write back that we will stop. The rest of the song is sung softly. Singing songs is now recommended as an outdoor activity, or when the children in the next room are elsewhere.

Note. There is fascinating background about 'Yankee Doodle.' Perhaps a student can research it and share the information with the class.

Summary
A carefully crafted environment of music's melody and harmony lends a unique component to the classroom setting. Background music mixed with quiet moments in the day provides a joy-filled atmosphere.

> *Music washes away from the soul the dust*
> *of everyday life.*
> Berthold Auerbach

1010.C THE POWER OF QUOTATIONS
Thanks to the invention of the alphabet, a person's thoughts from thousands of years ago are read today. This makes the alphabet a most amazing invention. The words of famous people from long ago lend authenticity and acceptance to today's ideas. Their inspiration impacts our lives.

Story
A high school principal believes in the power of words to influence student behavior. In 6 inch high letters, Dr. Jacobson has quotes painted throughout the hallways, gym, and lunchroom. Chosen to inspire, they are thought-provoking and challenging.

One high school student mentions the impact of a quote in the gym saying, "That quote really helps me. It makes sense, like it tells me what direction to take."

Be less curious about people and more curious about ideas.
Marie Curie

Summary

The power of a few succinct words speaks throughout time. Well-written quotes are clear, concise, compelling, and catchy. Quotations spur students to analyze and identify their implications. As students find and share their favorites, analysis and evaluation impacts their thought.

Note. The quotes in this book follow the copyright rules which require that they are from those who lived more than 50 years ago.

If everybody is thinking alike, then
someone isn't thinking.
George Patton

1010.D FRAGRANCE IN THE CLASSROOM

Story

In junior high, a favorite rebellious act of us 13-year-olds is removing our smelly gym sneakers in the next class. Winking at each other, we giggle as the smells waft around the room. Entering the room, the teacher says not a word. Smart teacher. By not reacting, she knows we will lose interest in our prank. She is right.

Based on the popularity of fragrances today, their uses and effects are listed on the Internet. Research says that organic grapefruit and orange scents can be safely sprayed in the classroom as they don't set off allergies. Sprayed lightly, they cancel unwanted odors brought in from gym class or recess.

Multi-use

A custodian, who refurbishes burnt-out cars, puts half grapefruits throughout the car's interior. He explains, "Grapefruit eliminates the smoke's acrid odor." The half grapefruits also work well when fireplace smoke fills our home. A co-teacher sprays the grapefruit scent just before the children arrive in the morning to create a welcoming freshness.

The orange scent is claimed to increase intelligence. Logically speaking, if this fact is true, school hallways and classrooms will smell like orange groves. The orange scent is rather gentle and t a favorite. Entering the room, the students' noses notice, and faces smile.

Note. To experiment with fragrances is fun. But to clear the air, an open window and nearby fan work just as well.
Note. White vinegar sprayed lightly around the classroom also cancels odors as well as fragrances that don't work out.

Observation

Spiders who spin their webs around front and back doors during the warm seasons do not like the orange scent. After scrubbing the area, it's lightly sprayed. The spiders stay away for up to six months. This does not work for students.

Summary

Other scents said to enhance learning include peppermint, citrus, and lavender. Internet research explains a fragrance attaches itself to an important event or activity. Hmm. If a chocolate scent is used while memorizing multiplication facts, will it improve memory? Let us pause and think. Will this be like the music, not recalled unless the scent is present? Are M&Ms necessary to eat during a multiplication fact test? Or, if you are eating chocolate, do you recall a multiplication fact? It is true, ideas for teaching are never boring.

Jasmine, the name of which symbolizes fragrance,
is the emblem of delicacy and elegance.
Dorothea Dix

1010.E ROOM DESIGN

With today's large tables, fake Ficus trees, skinny pole lamps, mobiles, posters, music, and artwork, classroom designs are as unique as the teacher's creativity. Bulletin boards covered in student work, posters, and positive messages abound. However, these 'papers' can become a 'chatter' of visual distractions that reduce children's ability to complete assignments.

Story

"I don't understand," says Shawn's mom. "He's been looking forward to science camp all spring. After 2 classes, he doesn't want to go again." The next morning, we accompany Shawn to his class. Stepping into the classroom, he immediately darts under a large table and refuses to come out. His teacher explains, "Yesterday, he and another boy stayed under there for the entire class."

Looking around the room, Shawn's 'problem' becomes obvious. Mobiles hang from the ceiling, posters cover the walls, and a collection of planet photos fills the whiteboard. For Shawn, his ability to process new ideas can't function. He needs to look away from visual distractors. This room is overwhelming.

His teacher agrees to provide a few 'white spaces' to reduce the boys' stressful reaction to the overwhelming room decorations . Shawn happily finishes his summer class.

Note. Shawn's learn-think-process styles are KAV.
1011.H HOW LEARNING HAPPENS - AVK

Story
A 1st grader asks to turn her desk against the wall. She wants to face away from the class activities. Forming a mini office, the sheltered arrangement allows her to complete her assignments with less distractions.

Bolted down furniture
Being an older building, Morris Elementary School's bolted-down seats and desks are arranged in rows. Throughout the grades, the students sit alphabetically. Telling my grandmother about the seat assignments, she remarks that the same rows and desks were in her one-room schoolhouse in 1901.

Moveable furniture
A.* The first class of 4th graders sit at desks with seats attached. To take out a pencil or notebook, the top is opened upward. As a result, many a book lands on the floor. The 21 desks are divided into 2 groups. Angled toward the teacher's desk, student attention is better focused.

The first night, the custodian put the desks back into rows. The next morning, we rearrange them. The second night, the desks again become rows. We catch on. Before going home, we create rows so sweeping is easier. In the morning, we angle the desks again.

B.* Over time, desks and chairs become two separate pieces of furniture, and arrangement options pop. When the school year begins, the desks are set in traditional rows facing forward. After a few weeks, the students' self-discipline improves. Now clusters of 2 and 4 desks become the preferred arrangement as this set-up creates lots of open space.

C.* Four desks facing each other have a major drawback - the easy ability to chat. Who would have guessed? One year, a student's dad made attractive, framed Masonite boards that sit between the 4 desks just high enough to separate the students into 2 and 2. Angled toward the front of the room, the chalkboard is easily visible. Students treat their sitting area as an office cubicle by posting items on the Masonite. Being a small class of 21, this arrangement works well.

Story
During tests, the students are taught a 'test cover technique'- keep a blank paper over their answers. A college experience taught this technique.

The student behind me copies my test answers. When the tests come back, she's failed. Hollering, she tells the class she copied, so why do I pass, and she doesn't? Comparing our tests, she discovers she miscopied a column of answers.

At the end of the class, the professor is questioned, "Why didn't you stop her" His reply, "I thought you wanted her to copy you. Your answer sheet wasn't covered." To ensure accurate test results in the future, students are taught to cover their answer sheets.

The group meeting
For me, the most delightful seating arrangement is students sitting on the floor facing the teacher on a chair. Seated close together, it's easy to communicate. From 1st to 5th graders, children enjoy the camaraderie of this arrangement.

Summary
Room arrangements fit the style of the teacher, the needs of the students and the activity. Today, when students sit at computers, their desks are arranged in rows. Different times, different arrangements. Wait! Didn't we start with rows?

1010.F A PRINCIPAL'S IMPACT
Mr. Steitzer is our new elementary principal. Near the end of the year, he

calls me into his office. At the time, I am teaching enrichment activities to small groups. He has a question about student intelligence.

Spreading the school's ITBS scores across his desk, he asks, "Can you explain why past low scoring students suddenly improve so dramatically on this year's tests?"

Asked what he did differently after becoming principal in our building, he explains. "Artwork found in the school attic is hung in the hallways. A 15 foot mural from the 1930's fills the school entrance hall. Sparkling clean halls are important to me. The custodians must immediately sweep the hallways after the students arrive - especially during Iowa's winter weather.

Working with the teachers, we upgrade expectations for good behavior and assignments finished on time. Parents are informed that students are to be dropped off when the school opens. No longer does anyone hang around the outside doors until school begins. With fair and enforced procedures, the school is peaceful."

The explanation
"Mr. Steitzer, you created an ideal learning environment of art, cleanliness, calmness, and clear expectations. As these are critical components to student success, your students' grades went up."

He is amazed at the power of the changes he'd implemented. They have obviously worked. He says, "I'll explain what happened to the district principals at our next meeting." He's discovered the key game changers for effective education.

Summary
Mr. Steitzer, taking strong stands, and working with willing teachers, and supportive parents contributed to student success.

An Executive Summary on the Internet, synthesizes research related to school leadership. It identifies the principal as key to student success. Investing in high quality leadership pays off.

Progress is impossible without change, and those who cannot change their minds cannot change anything.
George Bernard Shaw

In garden arrangement, as in all other kinds of decorative work, one not only has to acquire a knowledge of what to do, but also to gain some wisdom in perceiving when it is well to let alone.
Gertrude Jekyll

PART II
ATMOSPHERE

1010.G SILENT SIGNALS SPEAK LOUDLY

In warfare, soldiers on both sides establish unique communication techniques. In one ongoing battle, it is plain to the Americans that the enemy knows every move they are about to make. Who is telling the enemy their plans?

After a group discussion and quiet reflection, a soldier speaks up, "Have you noticed that the enemy hangs laundry outside their house every day? That's odd considering only a few people live in the house." He is right. The pattern of the hanging laundry communicates the Americans' plans. What is a powerful silent signal.

Story
While the 1st grade reading group is in session, the fake Fiscus tree suddenly falls over. A teacher's raised eyebrow toward the culprit tells him that he needs to take care of it. Quietly he comes over and whispers,

"Can Doug help me put it back up?" The teacher nods. With only a momentary interruption, the children continue to work.

Silent signals
Classroom signals can be simple. A smile. A nod. Thumbs up. A head shake. Raised eyebrows. A hand held up palm out. When they're combined with spoken directions, they develop meaning. Eventually, the nonverbal signals take over. The room is quieter, the children calmer.

> *Nothing strengthens authority so much as silence.*
> Leonardo da Vinci

1010.H GRATITUDE AND PRAISE
What makes a student happy? A teacher happy? Anybody happy? Praise and gratitude. Kind words are remembered years later and bring a smile to the face. Children 'go the extra mile' when they are happy. Words of praise are golden.

Praise that is light and easy is believable. "This class is awesome and on target!" obviously hits the mark when students glance at each other, nod, and smile. If a student is disruptive during class time, a finger points to the door to send the disorderly child out of the room. With discipline in the privacy of the hallway, the student is not unduly embarrassed. The class continues working, or listens carefully as the case might be.

Note. Discipline combined with gratitude for past good behavior turns the child in the right direction.
1008.D WARS BEGIN WITH DISAGREEMENTS – TRIBAL DISCIPLINE

Wordless praise can be a silent act that keeps the students quiet, yet feeling appreciated. Silent clapping, even a thumbs up, compliments the class for a good job. For self-congratulations, each child lifts up a hand and crosses it to pat the opposite shoulder.

Story

A colleague recalls this from her student teaching days. When speaking to the class, her lead teacher pulls her chair close to the front row desks and talks quietly. The class has to become as still as mice in order to hear her. Messages of needed discipline and loving compliments keeps their attention. I admire such a technique. How beloved this teacher must have been with her discipline centered in the quietude of loving kindness.

Quiet signals create a gentle atmosphere. In the hallways and lunchroom, all eyes turn toward the teacher for silent directions. Correcting poor behavior with silent signals allows the children to feel safe from loud words that shatter everyone's mood.

The Principal's role

Education research states that the school principal is key to the positive atmosphere of the school. (wallacefoundation.org) Our principal visits the classrooms every Friday. The building's open space concept of no walls takes him from one room directly into the next. His smile is broad. His compliments are for everyone. "You are a great class!" he booms out. "Learning is important! You have a fantastic teacher! Listen to her and learn! What a wonderful day you are having!" He makes a positive difference to all of us. Thank you, Mr. Rich.

Praise

Amazing! Fantastic! Wonderful! Terrific! Incredible! Phenomenal! Great idea! Fascinating! Beautiful! You've got it! Well said! Neatly done! Quite precise! Unique idea! A smiley face drawn on the board. Thumbs up. A happy note on the board to be read by students returning to the room.

Summary

Where praise and gratitude abound, children's willingness to work and share ideas is natural. Lovingkindess contributes to successful learning.

As the teacher models kind behavior, the students soon learn that there is something good to say to everyone.

1009.C ABCD'S OF KINDNESS

No act of kindness, no matter how small, is ever wasted.
Aesop

1010.I WILLINGNESS TO BE FAIR

"The world isn't fair," the fifth graders moan. "We feel discriminated against just because we're kids. Store clerks make us wait when we want to buy something. They take the grownups first."

Fairness
Every Monday, the next student based on the class list becomes the line leader for the week. The students complain further, "It takes too long to be a line leader." A truly coveted position! A brainstorming session is held to identify 'line up' options. Whoever is first on line, becomes the line leader.

Lineup ideas
- odd numbers one day, then even the next.
- favorite foods. Whoever likes almonds or licorice or purple…goes first. then comes the large group.
- favorite color or sport or flower or….

The children quickly learn to choose their friend's choice.

After 2 weeks, the class is tired of being fair in lining up and changing line leaders. They decide to let everyone stand on line wherever they want. It is an interesting reversal. The line leaders are again rotated alphabetically. No one says anything.

Summary
This class needed a sense of fairness. A teacher's willingness to listen and let children work out the problem allows them to feel heard and

understood. They are at peace. A heart of love makes a difference to the young people.

Story
The students complain that note passing is not allowed. A new method is suggested. The students decorate large business envelopes with their name and an 'address.' Stapled to the bulletin board by the door, personal notes are delivered to their post office during the day. At recess, they take them outside to read. The students' interest did not last long. It must be more fun to pass a note when the teacher isn't looking.

These men ask for just the same thing, fairness, and fairness only. This, so far as in my power, they and all others shall have.
Abraham Lincoln

1010.J HONESTY MADE EASY
As the 2nd graders are lining up for lunch, Suzy suddenly hollers out, "My lunch money is gone. It was in my desk. It's been stolen!" The students freeze. Stealing is a big deal in their world. Who did it?

The thought comes, don't let this become a big issue. As a 2nd year teacher, there is still a lot to learn about children, especially seven year olds. The goal is to get the money back with as few upsets as possible.

Immediately, the class is given a new line-up procedure. "As your row lines up, each of you come to me first and whisper in my ear 'yes' if you took the money, 'no' if you didn't."

Barely half the class is lined up and whispered "No" when Suzy rushes out of the coatroom announcing loudly, "I forgot! I brought my lunch today! I didn't have any money in my desk." She joins her class on line unaware of the commotion she's caused - mostly for her teacher! Totally baffled, I stare at Suzy. In a nano second, 'all is lost' changes to 'all is well.' Nonplussed the 2nd graders file quietly out of the room. Their relieved and subdued teacher follows.

The event is a good lesson. First, relax in the face of 'disasters' and realize the end of the world has not come. Second, ask detailed questions to clarify the problem. Third, use a quiet approach to solve the problem. The sudden idea of the 'whisper method' avoids mistaken accusations. Looking back, how would have the scenario unfolded if it was announced, "Everyone stay in your seats. We are not going to lunch until this money is returned!"

Upset children cannot think or process to find a solution. Kept in her seat, it might have been a while before Suzy recalls that she brought her lunch. Maybe we would still be waiting for the culprit to speak up.

Story
Another 2nd grade class. Another stolen item. This time it is a brand new brightly colored pencil. As the class lines up for recess, they are told, "Everyone is to whisper, 'yes' or 'no' as to taking the pencil. Even after someone whispers 'yes,' I will keep listening so no one knows who says 'yes.'"

Eventually one child whispers 'yes.' In the hallway, I button up his winter coat and whisper, "Before going outside, go back in the classroom and put the pencil on my desk." He does. After recess, we have a class discussion about honesty and friendship. Whispering keeps the situation low key. Young children make mistakes. In this case, the boy tends to be impulsive.

I call his mom and update her before he arrives home. She agrees to follow up with discipline.

Note. Calling a parent with a concern or compliment before a child arrives home coordinates school with home and builds trust between adults.

Summary
Honesty is a quality taught by example. Telling the students ahead of time that rain is expected and recess will be indoors, or the fire drill is scheduled for 10:30, creates a 'calm no surprises here' classroom. Honesty leads to trust.

> *Honesty is more than not lying. It is truth telling,*
> *truth speaking, truth living, and truth loving.*
> James E. Faust

1010.K THE TRUST FACTOR
With clearly explained criteria for an assignment, students work accurately, fearlessly, and independently. With no mine fields of unmentioned expectations, students trust the requirements.

Story
Although it's preferable to give students a heads up, the trust factor works best when it's previously established. In the following situation, the line leader is guiding the class down the hall toward the assembly room. Halfway there Joey suddenly stops. With a scared voice, says, "I don't feel good. I think I'm going to be sick."

A signal stops the line leader. The class is asked, "Who can walk quietly to the assembly without their teacher?" Hands fly up.

"Good. Follow our line leader. In the assembly room, follow the adult's directions as to where to sit. Behave as though your teacher is with you. I'll take Joey to the nurse's office." As we head to the clinic, the 1st graders march off confidently demonstrating their independence. I am proud of them.

A few minutes later, I hurriedly rejoin the class as the last students are taking their seats. Nodding to the vice principal who is seating them, it's hoped it looks as though there has been a slight delayed, but the teacher is nearby. The class watches. A thumbs up sign says, 'Well done.' Two fingers means a promise of two M&Ms back in the classroom. Happy smiles spread across their faces. Their independent behavior earns a reward.

Appreciation
Praise for good behavior builds student confidence. Gratitude given to the class who remembers to bring their homework back on time, walks down the hall properly, returns their permission slips the day after they are sent home reminds children they are trustworthy.

Story
Studying the pioneer days and how to maple syrup, one youngster speaks up. "There's a maple tree farm near my house. Their sign says tomorrow's the last day to take the tour."

Knowing the independence of these 2nd graders, the challenge is given, "Let's do it!" The class roars into action! Two students head to the office to confirm taking the trip. Once confirmed, the class president with the vice president call the tree farm to schedule a tour. The president then calls to schedule a school bus. (The transportation supervisor knows Beth. She'd scheduled a bus for the zoo field trip.)

With fellow students helping the class secretary, Emma writes the permission slip. She and the treasurer take it to the office for copies. Meanwhile, the students create a 'phone call tree' to remind each other to return the signed permission slips the next day. All is in place.

After the children arrive the next morning, it starts raining. Beth calls the tree farm and is told the tours are cancelled. She then cancels the bus. We continue our school day. I have often wondered. Did the children fully understand that they planned and executed field trip preparations within 2 hours? Obviously, they trusted their capabilities. Although the event might be forgotten, the process of independence is ingrained forever.

Summary

Trusting others is innate in children. As they learn to trust themselves, they learn their capabilities. Sharing the moments when they trust each other, trust becomes the foundation of effective action.

> *Love all, trust a few, do wrong to none.*
> William Shakespeare

1010.L TEACHER'S MOOD. STUDENTS' DAY.

What creates a joyful mood? A smile on someone's face, a compliment, a gift, or success on an assignment will do it.

Story
One morning, my headache is going from bad to worse. After the children are seated, they are told, "My day is not starting well. I have a bad headache. Will you please be especially helpful today?" The students rise to the challenge. They enjoy taking care of their teacher and being in charge of the class activities. The day's atmosphere is boosted by the excitement of independent accomplishments.

Students are mini-mirrors that reflect the mood of their classmates and the atmosphere. Their inner radar system bounces the energy around the room in a matter of minutes. To establish positive moods, teach them to pay attention to the joyful moments.

In the Fall, we walk to the playground under a row of autumn trees happily kicking the dry leaves into the air. In the Spring, we smell the same trees' flowers. A riddle, a joke, or playing 20 questions provides time for class-centered fun. A joyful classroom atmosphere reduces stress and contributes to student success.

Summary
Moods are delicate things. Children who arrive in the morning with new shoes or haircuts, smile cheerfully when a compliment is given. The class follows your joy-filled lead, and the classroom mood barometer goes up.

> *Sometimes if you begin to sing in a halfhearted mood, you can sing yourself up the ladder. Singing will often make the heart rise.*
> Charles Spurgeon

CHAPTER 10 IN CONCLUSION
CLASSROOM SETTING AND ATMOSPHERE

Enriched with art and music conducive to thinking, and an atmosphere of trust and gratitude, the classroom provides a safe space for learning and growing into adulthood. Quotations provide positive messages, silent signals preserve quietude. Student responsible for themselves brings success as the outcome.

A safe place for being a child happens in a structured environment. Where childhood is cherished, progress happens. The unknown future will be handled properly and fairly by a confident adult.

> *Education is not the filling of a pail, but the lighting of a fire.*
> William Butler Yeats

Chapter 11
A Plethora of Ideas

Perceive into and beyond the fundamentals

Topics
A. Use Plans B. Make Decisions C. Bloom 1,2.3
D. Bloom 4,5,6 E. Bloom's Chart F. Thinking Techniques
G. 2-D Graphic Designs H. AVK Learning I. 7 Intelligences

Introduction

To learn is to gain knowledge. We learn things by instruction, and by experience, and by observation. To learn is to acquire a skill. To learn is to receive intelligence.
Noah Webster's 1828 Dictionary

Children who use their intelligence, knowledge, understanding, wisdom, common sense, and 'street smarts' enjoy life's successes. Recognizing how thinking and learning happens, and their types of intelligence, the child's self-worth grows.

An authentic learner,
- makes plans and formulates decisions to create a firm foundation for daily living.
- applies a variety of graphics to deepen understanding and improve long term memory.
- infuses thinking techniques into school work and home life.
- analyzes questions based on Benjamin Bloom's 6 levels of thinking.
- understands how learning takes place and how they learn best.
- knows the 7 types of intelligences and which ones apply to them.

The result of being an authentic learner is a self-confident, responsible adult who contribute to and benefits society. The classroom of today is our nation of tomorrow. Becoming our future's success or failure, adults must teach the children thoroughly and well.

> *Power is given only to those who dare*
> *to lower themselves and pick it up.*
> *Only one thing matters, one thing;*
> *to be able to dare.*
> Fyodor Dostoesvsky

1011.A PLAN EVERYTHING

Written by the class, a 'plan of action' provides a detailed guideline for an activity. What might go wrong is identified and met with prearranged solutions embedded in the plan. As 'potential mistakes melt into nothingness,' successful endeavors are guaranteed.

Story
A 3rd grade class writes a plan to find the signs of Summer changing into Fall in the schoolyard. Seeking possible problems, they ask, "What if I fall down and get hurt?" The class decides to first look to see how bad it is, and then decide if going to the nurse's office can wait.

Sure enough, crossing the pavement to the yard, a young girl falls and scrapes her knee. Looking at it, she says, "It's not that bad. It can wait." Off she runs to join her class. The child clearly benefited from having a plan. She is calm in the face of adversity.

Be smarter
Research states that useful plans require well thought out details plus a clear understanding of those details.

    Basic Plan
    1* State the plan's purpose. Clearly stated, it sets the goal.
    2* Write a description. Expanded details show understanding.
    3* List the materials needed. 'Get materials' and 'clean up' are required steps.

4* List the steps to meet the goal. The procedure gets long as the students visualize the activity mentally and add details.

5* Identify possible problems and their solutions. Careful analysis of sources for materials and of each step of the procedure reveals possible missteps and clarifies solutions.

Plans save time. Alert to accuracy and aware of implications, success has a better chance of happening. Teams can practice writing plans about every day activities such as eating in the lunchroom, playing at recess, participating in art, music, and PE. A plan demands thorough thinking. Based on principles, it infuses children's behavior with courage and patience to try new activities.

Summary
With clear expectations and guidelines, an activity is completed in an orderly manner. Knowing what to do when things go wrong, students gain confidence in handling mistakes.

Note. Writing a detailed plan can be skipped if the class knows the basic procedures. Instead, focus on possible problems and solutions. When the whole process becomes clear, 'I've got this!' are the words of success. Several plans are used in Chapter 7.

A Plan
1. Set the purpose.
2. Explain the details.
3. List the materials.
4. Identify the steps.
5. Review and make corrections and addtions.

If it's your job to eat a frog,
it's best to do it first thing in the morning.
And if it's your job to eat two frogs,
it's best to eat the biggest one first.
Mark Twain

... now there's a plan! :)

1011.B MAKE GOOD DECISIONS
Overview
This process takes time and is a complete lesson in itself. Discussion of
the options and probing questions further clarifies the key question.

Steps
1* What is the <u>decision</u> about? Clarify this <u>question</u> thoroughly.
2* Consider the possible <u>answers/solutions/options.</u> If it's obvious a
solution is useless, save time, don't consider it.
3* Ask <u>probing questions</u>. Their answers point to the final decision.
4* <u>Defend</u> the final decision. Use the details of the probing questions
to explain which final answer is the best.

The possible solutions or options are on the left side. The probing
questions are written to match the Q1 to Q5.

Options	Q1	Q2	Q3	Q4	Q5	YES	NO
A							
B							
C							
D							
E							

The Main Question

A decision making lesson.
1008.K PACK A CONESTOGA WAGON

Summary
Decision making is an internalized response used to buy a candy bar or a new pair of shoes. Options weighed by good probing questions define the best decision.

Trust. Sometimes an answer is known before the decision making. Perhaps it's past experiences or an inner understanding that knows the final choice. This is called a gut response or intuition. Trust it.

Note. Research says a teacher makes over 1500 educational decisions per day. (www.teachthought.com) Like wow. It must be true - thinking takes place 400 times faster than we speak. (www.neurotray.com) Teaching is forever spontaneous.

> *A wise man makes his own decisions,*
> *an ignorant man follows public opinion.*
> Grantland Rice

1011.C THINK SMARTER WITH BLOOM 1,2,3
In the 1950's, Dr. Benjamin Bloom classified cognitive thinking into 6 levels. Today, the online New World Encyclopedia explains the effect of his research on education.

Bloom's research shows that both the classroom setting and the child's home improve a child's capabilities. Dr. Bloom's work changes 'how to teach' in the world of education. His research proves that it is not an inborn genius that leads to success in life, but rather …(it takes) "years of committed effort before achieving meaningful recognition." (paraphrase) In this chapter, Bloom's research is develops higher levels of thinking based on a well-known fable.

Set Up

To learn how to use Bloom's thinking levels, students write questions based on a familiar story, *The Three Little Pigs*. Writing questions from simple to complex, cognitive thinking reaches higher levels. Focused, and in deep thought, there is a stillness in the undisturbed thinking of a child.

To Begin

A detailed story of the 'Three Little Pigs' is read aloud. The students then use the summary below to write Bloom's cognitive questions. This makes the classwork consistent.

The Three Little Pigs

Mama Pig decides it is time to send her three piglets into the world to earn their fortune. Leaving home, they decide to build houses. As each pig has his own idea for a house, they build their own. The first pig builds a house of straw and string. The second pig uses sticks and twine. The third pig creates his house of bricks and mortar.

In the nearby forest, lives a wolf. Watching the piglets run back and forth to build their homes, he gets very hungry. At last, the pigs go inside their homes to rest.

Marching over to the house of straw, Wolf shouts, "Little Pig, little Pig, let me come in!" The piglet, who correctly supposes he will be eaten, says, "No, no, not by the hair of my chinny chin chin!"

Wolf yells, "Then I'll huff, and I'll puff, and I'll blow your house down!" *Puff! Huff!* As the straw house collapses into a heap, the first pig runs to his brother's brick house. Even hungrier, Wolf rushes to the house of sticks. His demand and the pig's answer are the same. Wolf starts huffing and puffing against the door. As the house collapses inward, the second pig runs to his brother's brick house.

Starving, Wolf races toward the brick house with his stomach growling. However, he decides to change his tactics to a more pleasant approach. He tries to trick the 3 pigs into leaving the house. First, he offers an invitation to the County Fair. Next, he offers a new and larger forest home for them to live in. The third pig outsmarts him every time. At last, Wolf disappears into the forest still looking for something to eat.

The pigs? They live happily ever after building homes for their animal friends. To keep themselves safe, they build a 2 bedroom addition onto the brick house.

For writing cognitive questions, a chart of Bloom's basic taxonomy is posted and a handout provided. We start with the simplest level, knowledge.

BLOOM'S TAXONOMY
levels of Cognitive Thinking

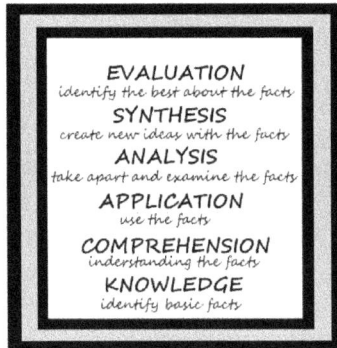

EVALUATION
identify the best about the facts
SYNTHESIS
create new ideas with the facts
ANALYSIS
take apart and examine the facts
APPLICATION
use the facts
COMPREHENSION
understanding the facts
KNOWLEDGE
identify basic facts

Thinking Level 1
Knowledge
Knowledge is a collection of basic facts such as dates, time, number of, where, and when,

TEACHER "To learn how to write knowledge questions, let's use the summary of *The Three Little Pigs*. Bloom's thinking chart will guide us. Level one is at the bottom. What does it say?"
STUDENTS "Knowledge. Identify basic facts."

TEACHER "Yes. What are some story facts?
STUDENTS "…wolf lives in the forest…the houses are different."
1004.E DOUBLE READING CIRCLES - validation

TEACHER "Choose one story fact. With your study partner, write a question with the fact as the answer. "
STUDENTS
   - How many pigs are in the story? (4)
   - What did the first pig use to build his house? (straw and string)
   - What did the wolf say first? ("Little Pig, little Pig, let me come in.")

Thinking Level 2
Comprehension
Clarify facts. Explain a fact so it is understood.

TEACHER "Bloom's thinking level 2 is comprehension. Find a fact that needs explaining. Write a question and answer that proves you understand what is said in the story.
STUDENTS
- What does it mean to 'find your fortune'? (The pigs were not going to live at home anymore. They are on their own. They will find jobs.)
- Why did the pigs build a house? (To protect them from the wolf. So they don't get wet when it rains. Mama Pig sent them out of their childhood home.)
- What makes a strong house? (Bricks and mortar - hard)

Thinking Level 3
*Application

Ask a question to figure out new information.

TEACHER "Bloom's application level focuses on figuring out new information. Let's ask questions that show how a fact is used."
This level includes implications which are open-ended and have lots of answers.

STUDENTS
-Why don't the pigs build the same house?
> There isn't enough of one material. The pigs have different ideas of safety. They have different amounts of money to buy the materials.

-Why are the pigs building houses?
> They can't live at their mother's house anymore.

-Why do 2 houses not protect the pigs?
> The straw house is too bendy, so the thin string doesn't hold it together very well.
> The sticks don't fit together, and the twine isn't strong enough to keep them together.

-Why is the 3rd pig's house the best?
> Bricks are heavy and mortar is like cement, so the house is very strong.

-How else could the wolf get into the houses?
> Knock down the doors with a big stick. Take the roof apart.

Summary
When students write questions about information,
- understanding is clearer.
- student thinking is 100% involved.
- thinking is purposeful.
- it's easier to choose the correct answer on a test.
- how questions and answers interact is understood.

Thinking is the hardest work there is, which is probably the reason so few engage in it.
Thomas Edison

Judge a man by his questions rather than his answers.
Voltaire

1011.F THINK SMARTER WITH BLOOM 4,5,6

Understanding these 3 higher cognitive levels, students learn curriculum faster and more thoroughly. Going beyond memorization to *contemplation and consideration*, recall is improved. A child who thinks hard about information, remembers it. This is why an eventful day is better remembered than a regular day.

> *All the forces in the world are not so powerful*
> *as an idea whose time has come.*
> Victor Hugo

1011.F Thinking with Bloom 4,5,6
The Three Little Pigs continue

Thinking Level 4
Analysis
Take a fact apart and figure out how the parts perform and interact.

TEACHER "Look over the *Little Pigs* summary, what details are not explained in the story?" (record answers)
STUDENTS "What are the steps to building a house? Why does a house fall over - or not? Why does the wolf want to eat pigs, and not forest animals? Why is the wolf's huffing and puffing so strong? Why doesn't he push the houses over?"
TEACHER "Write an analysis question and its answer. Work with your study partner."

> *It takes a very unusual mind to undertake*
> *the analysis of the obvious.*
> Alfred North Whitehead

Thinking Level 5
Synthesis
Use basic facts to create new interpretations or creative projects.

TEACHER "Synthesis is next. Look at the chart of our 2-D Graphics.
How can one be used to *interpret* the story information in a new way?"
STUDENTS "....
   - Diagram one of the houses and label it. Add new details.
   - Make a graph to show the types and amounts of materials used to
   build the houses and/or their costs.
   - Draw and label the steps to getting materials and building a house.
   - Use story details to draw a map showing the layout of the story.
   Add new additions that fit the story."
1011.C 2-D GRAPHIC DESIGNS - shows a 3 pigs map

Synthesis activities
TEACHER "Review the story again. What *inventions or projects* change
the story?"
STUDENTS
   - Design a new home for all 3 pigs.
   - Design a machine for the wolf so he can blast harder when he huffs
   and puffs.
   - Mama Pig writes a booklet about ways to seek a fortune.

Poetry is the synthesis of hyacinths and biscuits.
Carl Sandburg

Thinking Level 6
Evaluation
Ask questions to determine a fact's accuracy and its value.

TEACHER "Review the story. Write questions will decide the value of an
event?"
STUDENTS

-If Mama Pig wants her piglets to succeed in the world, what questions should she ask them?

-If a contractor checks the pigs' houses for safety and usefulness, what questions does he ask?

Summary

To understand an idea, dissect the information and examine its parts and their relationships. To create an invention, consider its use. Use evaluation questions to decide the value of an idea. Study teams support creative thinking.

1002.G THE ROMAN EMPIRE

When I am getting ready to reason with a man,
I spend one-third of my time thinking about myself
and what I am going to say and
two-thirds about him and what he is going to say.
Abraham Lincon

1011.E BLOOM'S CHART

Bloom's Cognitive Thinking

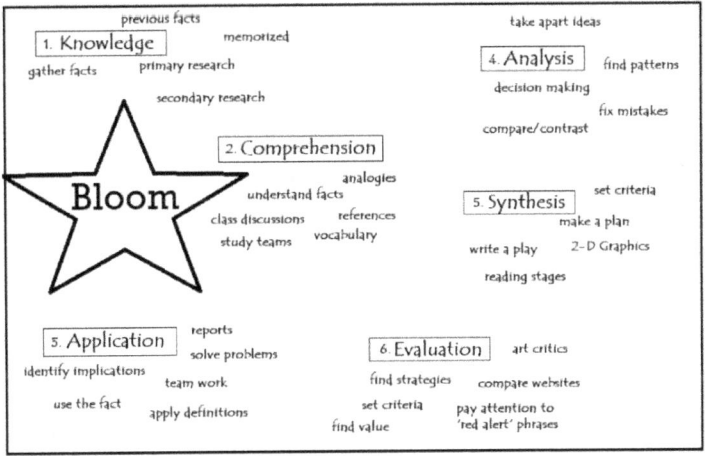

1011.F THINK TANK TECHNIQUES

A 'think tank' is a group of experts who focus their thinking on a single topic. These 7 techniques are used by a confident, expert thinker. Each technique shines its light on lesson examples and proves its application to be worthwhile. The student becomes a better thinker.

Thinking Technique 1
Analysis

Analysis takes ideas apart to examine the details as well as compare and contrast them. Analysis identifies the steps to create an outline or figure out the parts of a subject such 'What components make a pond?' For the learner, grasping the ideas behind smaller elements, the larger one gains clarity. Persistence underlies this work.

Analysis questions to be applied to a complex idea
What does a specific part tell you? What is its definition? Does another example come to mind? How do the parts work together? What is the role of each part? Is there a new way of using the part? Can the part be exchanged for a different one? Can it be modified to be more effective?

Applying analytical thinking to take a school assignment apart makes it easier to understand. It makes classroom activities easier to do. The process of planning and decision making rests heavily on analysis.

These activities focus on examining the parts of the whole.
1003.H TWENTY QUESTIONS. TERRIFIC THINKERS
1009.A ONE MINUTE TO A CLEAN CLASSROOM
1011.G 2-D GRAPHIC DESIGNS

Thinking Technique 2
Brainstorming

This is a highly creative procedure. The goal is lots of responses.
A broad based question releases thought to jump from place to place.
Totally opposite of careful logical thinking, one never knows where the

next idea will lead. Sound familiar? It's an open-ended question. As a guideline, tell the students whether imaginative answers are acceptable. For instance, Is a unicorn to be considered a forest animal?

To establish immediacy for every child, tell study teams to discuss the question first, then involve the class.
1005.F THIRD GRADERS. FIRST TIME WRITERS.
1007.J THE ARCTIC OR THE POLAR BEAR?

Thinking Technique 3
Compare/Contrast
To compare and contrast two or more objects, students examine them for similarities (compare) and differences (contrast).

For example. During the editing lesson, 'compliments for a job well done' are contrasted with 'helpful hints for improvement.' Honesty filled with compassion allows student help to be useful and supportive, not overbearing.
1002.D STUDENTS AS EDITORS
1006.I COMPARE FRACTIONS

Editing	
Compliments	Critiques
Title has the main idea	Title doesn't relate.
Detail fits topic	Detail is too broad
Vocabulary is interesting	Needs unique words
Spelling is excellent	Speling needs correcting
Ending is clear	End fades away
Note. Give exact examples of thse ideas.	

Thinking Technique 4
Implications
*Reading for beginners is a decoding process. The ideas behind the words must be learned.
*As students read at higher levels, they consider the effects of the facts.
*Studying the implications of historical events clarifies history.

This proverb reminds us to consider long range implications.

For the Want of a Two Penny Nail
For the want of a nail, a shoe was lost;
For want of a shoe, a horse was lost;
For want of a horse, a rider was lost;
For want of a rider, a message was lost;
For want of a message, a battle was lost;
For want of a battle, the kingdom was lost.
And all for the want of a two penny nail.

Updated by George Herbert in 1640
and later by Benjamin Franklin in 1758.

In formulating a plan or a decision, *implications* need to be automatically considered. It would have served our 19 year old well to consider the effects if his unique decision at the beginning of his high school freshman year.
1004.B IMPLICATIONS – THE MILLER
1007.D A BAT. A SNAKE. THE FISH.
1012.A NINETEEN YEARS OLD. NO DIPLOMA.

Thinking Technique 5
Organization
These examples are ways and reasons for organization to be taught to students. An organized child is a cheerful child. Everything is in its place and easily accessible.

*Organize before beginning a project, and the activity s smoothly. (science investigations)
*Organize school materials (desks and lockers) to avoid wasting time searching for an item.
*Clear, organized directions lead to clear expectations and results.
1008.F BECOME AN EXPERT

Thinking Technique 6
Predict
What comes next in a number series such as 2,4,6…? What does osmosis do to paper towel strips dipped in water with food coloring?
1007.G WHAT COLORS MAKE FOOD COLORING?

Predictions expand students' thinking beyond rote memory to the top of Bloom's cognitive thinking skills - synthesis and evaluation. When students start a math problem, predicting or estimating the answer first tells them whether their answer is 'probably right.'

Predicting is based on correct facts. Consider the possibility of bad weather on the day of the field trip, and we ask, "What do we do if it rains?" Then, in the calm moment of planning, backup procedures are included.
1003.G TWO PERSON INDOOR GAMES
1003.H 20 QUESTIONS. TERRIFIC THINKERS!
1007.B HOW MANY LEAVES ON A TREE?

Thinking Technique *7
Problem Solve
Solving 'real life' problems in the classroom, and mysteries in books, prepares students to handle their future problems with confidence. Questions that define the problem and possibilities for solutions becomes automatic.
1003.I SOLVE MYSTERIES

As students trust their ability to solve a problem, they develop self-confidence and certainty. The 'planning process' taught in Chapter 8 identifies 'hidden problems.' Creative thinking is developed.

Simple problems such as choosing which clothes to wear or fixing a snack or keeping dry in a rainstorm or forgetting homework at home, are met and mastered by the child who is a decisive problem solver.

1010.I Willingness To Be Fair
1011.A Reduce Problems. Plan First.

Summary
Think Tank Techniques expand a short lesson, enrich a review for a test, and enrich familiar information. Students who think become better learners and effective assistant teachers. This is true learning.

1001.A Save the Substitute
1008.G The Roman Empire

> *If you think you can do a thing, or you think you*
> *cannot do a thing, you are right.*
> Henry Ford

1011.G 2-D Graphic Designs
Condensing information from several pages in a textbook onto a single page of key facts makes seeing the overall picture easier. This analysis deepens understanding and makes facts more easily remembered. Test scores improve. Graphics have a unique role in learning.

To encourage students to ask questions, make the first type of graphic with the class. Afterwards, whether copying the class graphic with modifications or creating a new one individually, students add the example to their portfolio. Copying to learn is a first step in comprehension.

These 7 graphic designs focus on details and connections between facts. For the students, working in teams helps them think through the type of graphic. Becoming familiar with a graphic, they easily apply it to new information. Graphics are powerful ways to learn and understand.

Chart
A chart lists information or steps.
It may be an alphabetized vocabulary list or the steps to solve a

math problem. Posting the rules for grammar or directions for a science investigation keeps students alert. A chart helps children remember.

A multiplication tactic chart

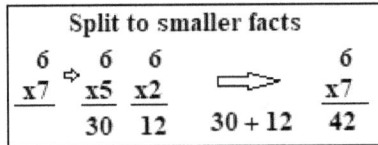

Split to smaller facts			

$$6 \Rightarrow \begin{array}{cc} 6 & 6 \\ \underline{\times 5} & \underline{\times 2} \\ 30 & 12 \end{array} \quad \Rightarrow \quad 30 + 12 \qquad \begin{array}{c} 6 \\ \underline{\times 7} \\ 42 \end{array}$$

Diagram

A diagram identifies the parts of an object or describes a set up for an activity. Labels describe the object or action. If a complex diagram is handed out, encourage students to add notes during the introduction or review.

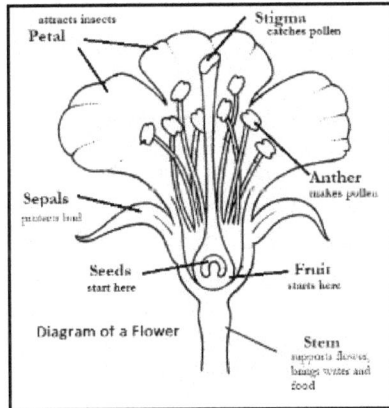

Diagram of a Flower

This diagram of the parts of this flower explains how a seed is made.

Drawing

For a lecture, each fact becomes an icon. Labeled and similar ideas connected by lines, the orderly approach provides clarity for a complex presentation. Visual learners find a drawing easier to study than pages of written information. If the drawing is based on reading a textbook, page numbers are included next to the icon.

This drawing is based on the frog lesson in Chapter 5.
1005. C FROG SENTENCES: 2 TO 22 WORDS

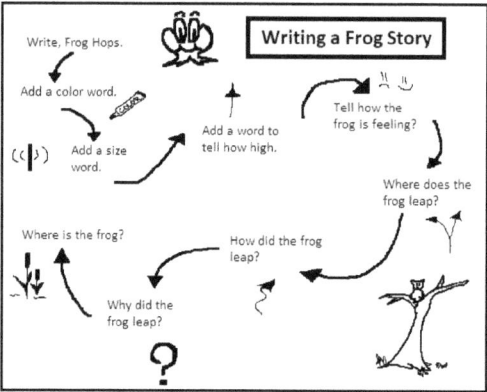

Story
The sister of a tutoring student arrives to pick him up. Asked if she'd like a quick study tip, she answers with a polite smile, "I don't need study help, I already get A's. Plus, I don't like to draw pictures like my brother does." I answer, "Then you aren't a visual learner. My tip to you is 'To make studying easier, write questions and answers about the information.' You'll learn even faster than you do now."

Two weeks later, she stops in again to express gratitude. "Thanks! That worked. I did study faster, and I still got an 'A'!" She learns best with words, whereas her brother learns best with pictures.

Map
A bird's eye view of a story puts the details into context. This map of the

"Three Little Pigs" includes details that *aren't in the story*. Creative thinking shows the sources for the building materials. A brick factory, the woods, and a farm are located near the correct house. They add depth to the story and make the map more interesting.

Interpretations

Putting Mama's house behind rows of bushes explains why the wolf doesn't visit her house. The location of the forest explains why the first pig is first. It would be incorrect if the map shows the third pig lived next door to the first pig. Reasoning leads to a more interesting map of many details.

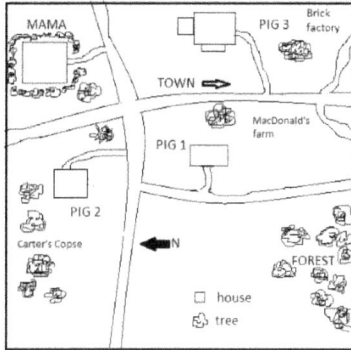

Time Line

Drawing the steps in the growth of a plant and labeling its parts, patterns and details are revealed. If the length of time isn't known, add imaginary dates. This time line can be used to write a story about a seed growing.

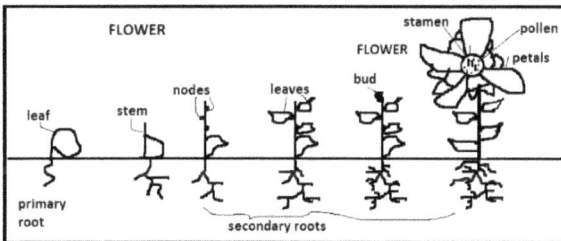

Web or Cluster ... aka Mind Map

*Lecture Web

During a class lecture, draw a web of icons on the board to show the connections between the ideas. If the ideas must be in order, start from the *top right* and move *clockwise* in a circle.

*Research Web

Because this 'wolf web,' is based on research, the references are listed at the bottom. The letter of the reference and its page number are placed next to each fact. The students identify the research ideas (words in the bubbles) before the specific facts are found. Writing the report is easy as the paragraphs and details are already clustered.

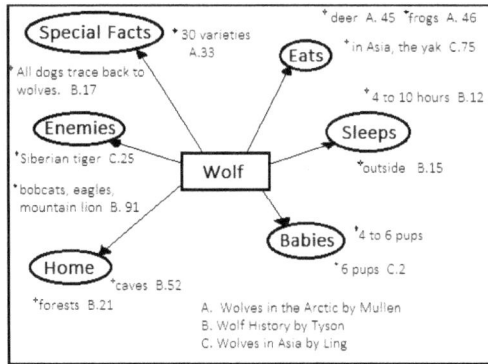

*Vocabulary web

As students contribute vocabulary for an activity, cluster similar words on the board so they are easier for the children to find. Use diversity, unique, and variety in Chapter one to encourage ideas.

Summary

A 2-D Graphic on a single page provides a detailed overview of a large amount of information. Dissecting ideas for the graphic focuses on the details of the larger idea. Rearranging them into the new design contributes to authentic learning.

After making the graphics, the children save their work. With a personalized collection of the 7 graphics, students have useful references for later assignments.

Get the habit of analysis - analysis will in time enable synthesis
to become your habit of mind.
Frank Lloyd Wright

1011.H HOW LEARNING HAPPENS - AVK

We observe what is around us by using our physical senses. Our ears *listen,* our eyes *see,* and we are *alert to movement.* This is referred to as a style of learning - auditory A, visual V, and kinesthetic K.

Auditory Learner

This learner listens and recalls precisely what is said. Information is easily recalled on a test. The auditory child learns best with discussions and collaboration, a dramatic voice, and interesting vocabulary.

Visual Learner

This learner stares intently at objects or information written on the board. Consider a list of important facts or directions, a 2-D Graphic, an outline of the chapter facts, an agenda. This style learns best with mind maps. graphics, pictures, anything that can be seen.

Kinesthetic Learner

This learner refers movement. This style wants to act out an idea, hear the description of an action story whose details can be seen mentally.

Emotions and feelings play a large role for the K learner. If the student likes the teacher, and vice versa, learning is more likely.

Another aspect for K to connect to learning is the sense of touch such as holding a pioneer object while listening to an explanation. This improves K's memory.

Summary
How is it possible to teach using 3 styles of learning? Include stories large and small. Every AVK learner easily recalls a story.
    *The drama of a voice reading aloud, its pauses and interesting words connect to the Auditory learner.
    *Descriptions of story events and characters with color and details connect to the Visual learner.
    *Action events and positive moods connect to the Kinesthetic learner.

With stories, students find it easier to pay attention. Grades improve. Success happens.

You may have heard that the whole world is made up of atoms and molecules, but it's really made up of stories....
William Turner

1011.I WHAT'S YOUR INTELLIGENCE?
After a 2 year worldwide research project, Dr. Howard Gardner of Harvard University identified 7 intelligences. They are published in his book *Frames of Mind: The Theory of Multiple Intelligences.* More books are now available.

The 7 intelligences are linguistic, mathematical, musical, bodily-kinesthetic, spatial, interpersonal and intrapersonal.
The following brief overviews simplify the key aspects. In-depth details and recent research are on the Internet.

The Wordsmith   Linguistic Intelligence

The Wordsmith uses verbal techniques in speaking and writing. Writing a complex sentence with many ideas, including creative analogies and interesting comparisons plus a super-large and complex vocabulary is normal. Poetry writing may be a favorite pastime as are conversations with friends. This thinker loves words.

The Number Wizard   Mathematical Intelligence

A Number Wizard is intuitive in solving math problems. Solutions to math challenges come quickly, easily, and often creatively. Answers may be known before the math is done, yet prove logically correct when figured out with math rules. This thinker finds more than one way to solve a number problem. This thinker includes orderliness and reason.

Sound Whiz   Musical Intelligence

With a fine-tuned ear, this thinker listens - then easily reproduces - melody, rhythm, and harmony on an instrument. In fact, on several types of instruments. With an ear for perfect pitch, the smallest variance in voice and music is discerned. With this alertness to nuances in sound, languages are easily learned, sometimes quite a few. Think of this intelligence in an orchestra, music albums, and translators between languages. This thinker includes harmony and spontaneity.

Whirling Winds   Bodily-Kinesthetic Intelligence

Whether involved in small movements such as quilting and playing a game of croquet or large ones such as walking over Niagara Falls on a cable, Whirlwind's ability to 'move in space' is both simple and fluid for this thinker. As an expert in sports or superb in acting, this intelligence develops precise movements needed for exceptional success. Think bocci ball, rock climbing, and surfing. This thinker includes grace and strength.

Painter and Chisler   Visual-Spatial Intelligence

A painting is a 2 dimensional reflection of the world shown either exactly or imaginatively. From murals to mini-paintings on jewelry, the painter sees the world two dimensionally.

A 3-D object such as a sculpture is shown front, back, and around. This thinker's careers include woodworking and construction, brain surgeon, and the civil engineer designing buildings and bridges. Taking apart a clock or a toy to see how it works inside, this thinker may invent a new one. This thinker includes creativity and beauty.

The Philosopher   Intra-Personal Intelligence

The Philosopher thinks in detail about everything. As a deep thinker, the preferred activity in life is understanding why and how the world works. While seeming to waste time staring into space, a whirlwind of ideas is being thought about, combined, and kept or discarded at lightning speed. This intelligence is often willing to consider new ideas in order to better understand another idea. The Philosopher includes insight, intuition, and intellect.

Note. This thinker contributes positive ideas to the world's behavior patterns including the last 3000 years. What an impact for this thinker.

People-Centered   Inter-Personal Intelligence

With detailed and carefree discussions, this thinker is highly sociable, and connects easily to a group. This thinker creates 'an effective force' in solving group problems. People-centered, they are often leaders in companies and in the world. This thinker includes a delightful friendliness and enjoyment of others.

How to teach to the 7 intelligences.
All types intelligences have one thing in common - they use thinking skills.. To provide a lesson for all 7 intelligences, use the thinking skills found in this chapter and in other educational resources.

Note. Some intelligences sound similar to the learning styles. (auditory, visual, kinesthetic.) However, a learning style is not the same as a high intelligence. A linguistic intelligence possesses abilities far beyond an auditory learner.

Summary
Each type of intelligence operates at a high level in a specific area of thought as compared to other people. According to Dr. Gardner, we all have *2 or 3 of these intelligences.* Students appreciate their self-worth when they know and demonstrate that they are highly intelligent in 2 or 3 of these 7 types of intelligences.

Story
Mary is the smallest child in the 5th grade. Very sweet, she often worries that she is doing something wrong. At that time, emphasizing the children's specific intelligences is not known. Classroom grades are the only basis for success.

After school is out, my daughter and I attend her piano recital. Skimming the list of the students, Mary's name is at the end next to the piano teacher's name. That day Mary's key intelligence is clear. Sitting with the teacher - a huge privilege - Mary performs the most amazing piano renditions. She, too, is a brilliant thinker.

Talent hits a target no one else can hit;
genius hits a target no one else can see.
Alfred Schopenhauer

CHAPTER 11 IN CONCLUSION
A PLETHORA OF IDEAS

Children challenged by interesting school lessons at which they succeed gain confidence , independence, and the understanding of their true self-worth. Developing into authentic learners, they -
- create effective plans.
- make smart decisions.
- ask high level questions and evaluate the results and implications. .
- identify and use their style of learning.
- evaluate and apply their intellectual capabilities confidently and consistently.
- appreciate and have compassion for others.

The classroom of today is our nation of tomorrow. Because our students become adults, we will see them and their ideas again. Self-confident, responsible adults contribute and benefit society with their talents.

The foundation of every government is
the education of its youth.
Diogenes

Chapter 12
#realstorieshappen

Respond with authority; continue with caring

Topics
A. No Diploma B. Change in Behavior C. Compassion for Richard
D. Alexa E. Handle Sickness F. An Amazing Question
G. Lesson Washout H. A Career Concludes

Introduction
Surprise, shock, and delight are part of a teacher's career. A sense of humor, a willingness to drop grudges immediately, and a quick and loving response to meet children's needs creates successful children and a safe classroom.

Handling each situation with thoughtfulness and compassion makes teaching a series of amazing experiences - suggesting that there are too many aspects to be taught in college classes.

> *The most worthwhile thing is to try to*
> *put happiness into the lives of others.*
> Robert Badon-Powell

1012.A NINETEEN YEARS OLD. NO ACADEMIC DIPLOMA.
"No one told me," Rick admits sheepishly. "A friend said it would be a great way to get through high school with almost no class work and no homework. All we had to do was pretend we were no longer smart and be put into a low achieving class."

It works. Rick enters high school with a sudden drop in mental ability. Tests don't locate the problem. After graduation, he watches his friends go off to college. Finding a job nearby, he rooms with 3 of them. Seeing their excitement in learning new courses, he wants to go to college. It is then he discovers he has an attendance diploma that does not support a college application.

"Watching my friends study their freshman courses, I know I can do the work. If I pass the GED - Graduate Education Development test - I can send it with my college application." He is right. Passing the GED provides the credits needed for a high school diploma.

Four years of high school can't be taught in one summer. But, I f Rick learns how a test question works and how to process information in a variety of ways, he will accomplish a small miracle - pass the GED test.

Note. GED test results also indicate which test areas - language arts social studies math science - need to be improved. Rick can re-take anything he fails. College admittance is the next hurdle.

Our academic basis for learning to think is J.D. Hirsch's book, *What Your 6th Grader Needs to Know*. Based on complex classical material, Rick learns to apply creative and academic study skills and write questions. The last skill will help him figure out answers about information he has not learned.
1011. C THINK WITH BLOOM 1,2,3
1011. D THINK WITH BLOOM 4,5,6

With persistent effort, Rick's learning curve accelerates. His friends' college work incentivizes him to keep to the high goal. In turn, they are highly interested in his new study techniques. Soon Rick is teaching them how to study their courses more efficiently. The benefit? Rick is learning his future freshman college material. His capabilities and confidence soar.

Summary
Yes, Rick passes the GED test. The following year he is in college with

his friends. His parents are dumbfounded by his chicanery while at the same time proud of his accomplishment against the odds of success.

What a 'life lesson' to learn so young. Taking the easy way out in the moment led to more challenges later. For me, his summer lessons reveal a key point - academics may be forgotten, but becoming a skilled thinker is a lifelong achievement.

> *Is there anyone so wise as to learn by the*
> *experiences of others?*
> Voltaire

1012.B CHANGE IN BEHAVIOR

The school year is over. Sitting at my desk completing a few papers, a young boy appears at the doorway. "Hi," he says tentatively. "I'm Tommy. I have you for my teacher next year."

Smiling, I answer, "Hi, Tommy. I look forward to having you in class. I know we will have a great year." He nods and leaves. I have no idea who Tommy is, but his hopeful smile touches my heart.

Summer is spent with my family, taking classes at the Des Moines Nature Center, and working in our vegetable garden. Not reading student folders over the summer, Tommy's past is unknown.

The first day of school, Tommy and his mother come into the classroom ahead of the other students. After welcoming them, his mother says that Tommy wants to tell me something.

Tommy begins. "I spent the summer planning a better way to behave in school. I always act up, and I don't want to be in trouble anymore. He points to a desk in front of the room. "I figure that the best place for me to sit is where I don't face anyone. Plus, I won't be near your desk when kids come up to talk to you."

His mother continues. "Tommy has never been able to control his impulsive behavior. His previous teachers and the school nurse suggested a calming drug, but for me, drugs are not the answer. I've tried diet and health changes. Nothing works." Her eyes fill with tears. "He wants to do well this year. He's planned all summer how to be better." After she leaves, it's clear that it has been a long 5 years for him and his family. Tommy sits down at the desk he's chosen.

Trusting Tommy's summer transformation, it's plain he will need the support of his classmates and school personnel. Our school is small and more than likely everyone knows about Tommy's misbehavior. Now I do, too. To help Tommy avoid being locked into his past, his classmates need an immediate update. After everyone is seated, the class is told about Tommy's new commitment.

"Tommy wants to change. He's planned all summer how to be better behaved. To give him that opportunity, we need to change, too. That means we don't bring up his past - not in this room, not in the school, nor on the playground, not anywhere. Who will help him make this change?" Hands fly up as the class commits their support.

While the class is in gym class, the office and lunch room staff, the principal, and when the opportunity arises, his past teachers are updated. Everyone is willing to support our 'new Tommy' and treat him as a 'regular kid.' Hearing about his past, I am grateful that over the summer Tommy mentally replayed the past, rejected it, and planned his new behaviors.

It is a marvelous year. Tommy discovers what it is like to be a regular school kid. Everyone helps him to start his new life. His family is thrilled and grateful. So am I.

When good men in any country cease their vigilance
and struggle, then bad men prevail.
Pearl .S. Buck

1012.C COMPASSION FOR RICHARD

The 3rd year is teaching 4th through 6th grade science classes. Most students follow the class rules, but one 6th grader loves interrupting the lesson with his viewpoints. Intelligent and with a good sense of humor, we are a captive audience for his spectacular perspectives.

One day, as the students line up to leave the room, a surprising side of him is revealed. Richard loses his cool. For an unknown reason, he decides to threaten his teacher. Dramatically he puts up his fists, takes a fighter's stance, and offers to beat me up. Mind you, he is a shade taller. His challenge puts the class on pause. Frozen in place, not one child moves. (At this time, there are no cell phones - no room phone either.)

Suddenly humor kicks in. Maybe it's because he is a likeable fellow and has never acted threateningly before. Taking a deep breath, and making sure he is paying attention, my body carefully and slowly moves to mimic his pose. Staring at his feet mine are moved to match his stance. Next, I bend my body like his and, glancing at his fists, put mine up the same way. Finally, I stick out my chin, look into his eyes, and sigh deeply. With exaggerated sadness, the words are said "I know I'm going to lose, but if it makes you happy, I'm willing to take you on." Richard bursts into laughter - as does the class. The threat of a fight melts into merriment.

This is not a recommended teaching technique. However, using humor to help this child out of a lose-lose situation saves both of us. As the 6th graders nonchalantly continue to their art class, they remind me of a class of 2nd graders.
1002.E WRITTEN AND PRODUCED BY 2ND GRADERS

A thought. "What did the students tell their parents that night about this event?

Humor is mankind's greatest blessing.
Mark Twain

1012.D ASK A 'LIVE' ALEXA
How far is it to the West Indies?
What are the cross-country routes the pioneers used?
Why does multiplying fractions make a smaller number?

5th grader Justin dutifully writes down his classmates' questions. His homework assignment is to find the answers. The following day, he reports the information to the class. The class delights in thinking of questions for him.

Why such unusual homework? Children with an extremely high IQ seldom need to study. Justin soaks up information like a sponge – seeming to know more than the teacher before the teacher teaches it. Justin is our class 'Alexa' before Alexa is invented.

A child with a high intelligence may find communication difficult as the other children don't process ideas as quickly. Playing a unique role for his class, Justin becomes popular, valued member of the group.
1011.I WHAT'S YOUR INTELLIGENCE?

The wise man doesn't give the right answers,
he poses the right questions.
Claude Levi-Strauss

1012.E A SICK CHILD
Returning from recess, the 2nd graders line up in the hallway for a drink of water. A boy suddenly says, "I feel sick," and then, he is.

Quickly the class is shepherded into the room. Phoning the office, a custodian is requested. At the same time, the sick child is given an empty waste basket to carry to the nurse's office. A friend goes with him for support. A short story is read to the class, then a lesson is given.

Talking with the custodian later, he's asked for something to eliminate the smell. He provides packets of powder similar to cat litter but with a sweeter smell. "Just sprinkle this on the mess and call for me." He grins, "I always show up fast before the other little ones get sick."

When older students say they are feeling sick, they are handed a 'quickly emptied' wastebasket and sent them to the nurse's office. That protects the school carpeting, and the child's reputation. No one wants friends to see them sick.

To handle sickness a plan of action is important. A speedy response, that special scented powder, and quickly emptied wastebasket works well. Over the years, there are only 3 'immediate' events. Children get sick. Be ready. Have compassion.

> *There is one consolation in being sick,*
> *and that is the possibility*
> *that you may recover to a better state*
> *than you were ever in before.*
> Henry David Thoreau

1012.F AN AMAZING QUESTION

"Why do you want to teach?" My college professor's question is startling. Preferring to garden, a landscape architect is first choice. Dad suggests being a teacher. "You're always organizing everyone."

One of the first answers is, "Because I love children." "Wrong!" shouts the professor. "That's not enough." The class is stunned. Teachers don't have to love children?

He continues, "A teacher needs to be effective. to teach students how to think and how to learn. It's not just curriculum. It's not all about love." It's clear. Our professor believes that teaching children how to think is important.

During the semester, each student presents an elementary grade lesson based on the professor's assignment. His critiques follow a pattern. "Remember the introduction. Hold back a question that's out of order, answer it later. Provide lots of examples. Make them think! Smile." His criteria is woven into my fraction lesson.

After Christmas, my lesson is given. Explaining how fractions work on a felt board is an amazing experience. As the class leaves the room, the professor says. "You did an excellent job. How did you do it?" The answer, "All semester how to write and present a meaningful lesson is made clear. Your critiques are consistent." He smiles. "You have your 'A.'"

The professor's teaching format is the foundation for this book - lots of examples, lots of details, stay focused, ask questions, teach students to think, smile. Caring about children is fundamental, but it's not enough. Authentic learning is based on thinking skills. Thank you, Mr. Professor.

Example is not the main thing in influencing others.
It is the only thing.
Albert Schweitzer

1012.G LESSON WASHOUT
The first lesson as a student teacher catches me off guard. After the teacher-mentor defines his expectations for introducing division to his 6th grade class, he suggests, "Begin by asking them to explain how multiplication works."

After the question is asked, the 6th graders slide down into their seats. No one knows how multiplication works. At that same moment, the superintendent steps into the room. With students disappearing out of sight and a 'very important person in the room,' opportunities for a successful lesson are fading fast.

Slowly setting the note cards down, and thinking fast, a new question is asked, "What do you know about adding numbers?" This technique of 'backing up to information previously learned in order to move forward' is learned in college. Switching to a question with a known answer, students gain confidence in participating.

The education professor is right. Knowing 'how to teach' is key. His education classes focus on the Socratic method, 'teach by asking questions.'

The math lesson continues with addition - combining numbers - which leads to multiplication - repetitive addition. The next day, division focuses on 'repetitive subtraction.' The 'surprise student response' changes the direction of the lesson. A backup procedure is good to have.

Note. After the superintendent's sudden visit, saying 'yes' to anyone asking to observe my teaching is comfortable. Sometimes a teacher or the principal needs to observe a lesson and critique it for a course they arc taking. For me, a personalized, nonthreatening process is more helpful than a formal education class. It's quicker, too.

On the flip side, by invitation, the county level professors bring their expertise into the classroom. Watching them demonstrate the newest teaching techniques, teachers stay up to date without attending a workshop.

Failure is simply the opportunity to begin again,
this time more intelligently.
Henry Ford

1012.H A CAREER CONCLUDES

Last Fall, a parent asks to have her son tutored. Due to new commitments and a longer commute, the previous year's lessons come to an end

A lecturer emphasizes, "If it's yours to do, nothing can stop you." Teaching is mine to do. Not even a passion for gardening stops it. Who chose the career doesn't matter. Being unprepared on the first day of teaching in front of 21 fourth graders doesn't matter.

To those who contributed to my journey - students, teachers, principals, district administrators, mentors, business trainers, my friends and, most of all, my family - I am most grateful. Your support was, and is, wonderful.

To the parents a huge thank you! From classroom volunteers to tutoring support, they bring a caring interest for their children's education. To those students who come to learn and bring their joy, intelligence, and humor to lighten the days, thank you.

Thank you to Dad, who sees the teaching potential, and to Mom, who supports it. Thank you, Dr. Jenkins, a language arts professor at South Side High School. You make learning a challenge and use humor to made it fun. To Mrs. Adler who proves that algebra, analyzed thoroughly, can be learned easily. To the State University of New York at Oswego, thank you for impacting my teaching career forever with the Socratic method of questioning. To Marycrest College in Iowa, which establishes a locally available Master's Degree program, thank you.

To my friends, co-workers, and mentors in the Cedar Rapids School System who teach this kinesthetic teacher new ways of teaching when her verbal skills are not enough, I thank you. A thank you to Dr. Richard Schultz who hires me to lead the development of the district science program from 1st to 6th grades. To Dr. Barton, who makes sure summer work in the business world strengthens confidence in teaching adults in our school district. Such total faith.

To the Iowa Conservation program, thank you for providing summer Nature courses to combine with classroom teaching. To Dr. Nicholas Colangelo at the University of Iowa who teaches teachers how to meet the needs of highly intelligent children - creative and academic - in the classroom. The 3 week course is a powerhouse of information that impacts teaching all children.

To Mr. Alan Kacere at the Palo Energy Plant who hires me to develop updated training materials for his instructors. To Dr. Hellman, who wants to provide his business trainers specific collaboration and interactive activities for their seminars.

To the principals of the Gwinnett School District in Georgia who encourage becoming a qualified teacher in Georgia. Shiloh Elementary School gives me an amazing 5 years for a classroom finale.

To my family who supports me. To my two dear children who take over their laundry and the house cleaning to free me to do my college homework. To my husband who takes care of the household while I take summer classes. He is a true support.

My deepest gratitude to the Supreme Being who guides, governs, and loves us all. For those many divine messages about how to teach the children, I am most grateful.

And to my dear Florrie, an abandoned cat who decides to live with me. This soft gray and white kitty sits in the children's laps when they come for tutoring. Her purrs provide a sense of peace and love for all of us.

> *It took me four years to learn to paint like Raphael,*
> *but a lifetime to paint like a child.*
> Pablo Picasso

CHAPTER 12 IN CONCLUSION
#REALSTORIESHAPPEN

Children need a calm and peaceful authority that confirms confidence in themselves. Praise, joy, gratitude, and a touch of humor handle the good and not so good things that happen during the school day.

May these stories contribute to an appreciation of teaching. Collect your experiences. The next generation of teachers develops a foundation for a free and moral country from those who are willing to share.

My best to everyone, and gratitude to all,

Miss Trudi

*The most satisfying thing in life is to have been able to give
a large part of one's self to another.*
Pierre Teilhard de Chardin

Miss Florrie

When the heart of the child is touched
by the love of the teacher,
true learning takes place

INDEX

A

Abby - shy child 1003.F
ABCD's kind… 1009.C
Ability level, read 1004.G
Ability teams 1009.E
'Add'tional math 1006.B
Addition 10 facts 1006.A
Alexa, ask 1012.D
Algebra - coins 1006.F
All the leaves? 1007.A
Alphabet words 1003.D
Analogue time 1006.G
Analysis 1011.D
Annie syllables 1003.A
Answer poem 1001.G
Ants, orig. rsrch 1007.I
Applica questions 1011.C
Arctic . bear 1007.J
Armistead, James 1008.F
Art in classroom 1010.A
Art - intelligence 1010.A
Assign numbers 1009.D
Auditory learning 1011.H
Authentic tching 1008.I
Authors, 1st gr. 1005.E
AVK learning 1011.H

B

Bach lesson 1001.A
Basic teach. steps 1001.B
Basic words 1003.D
Bat, snake, fish 1007.D
Bathroom 1006.G

Batteries, bulbs 1007.E
Battery and bulb 1007.E
Beanstalk Jack 1004.C
Bear, polar 1007.J
Behavior change 1012.B
Beloved discipline 1010.H
Bingo chips 1006.A
Bloom, 1,2,3 1011.C
Bloom, 4,5,6 1011.D
Bloom Chart 1011.E
Boat sailing 1001.D
Bobby.. frog 1005.C
Box…area 1006.E
Brainstorm 1011.F
Brainstorm voc. 1005.G
Bubbles 1007.F
Bug visitors 1007.C
Bulb, batteries 1007.E
Butterflies collab. 1002.B

C

Call a parent 1011.D
Capture curiosity 1001.D
Carpe Diem 1002.G
Carson, Dr. 1004.E
Cat litter 1012.E
Celebrate 1001.F
Chart 1011.G
Child spelling aide 1003.D
Children draw 1002.I
Church, painting 1010.A
Circle discipline 1008.C
Circle reading 1004.C
City park 1008.C

Clapping quietly 1010.G
Classical music 1010.B
Clean classroom 1009.A
Coins, algebra 1006.F
Collabora., Butter. 1002.B
Collaboration 1001.E
Color fractions 1006.H
Comet writing 1005.F
Compare 1011.F
Comp. questions 1011.C
Compassion 1012.C
Conestoga wagon 1008.K
Conjectures 1008.C
Connect ideas 1011.F
Conscious level 1011.H
Contrast 1011.F
Coordinating tchr 1010.G
Copy to write 1005.D
Costumes 1002.E
County profs 1012.G
Cover the test 1010.E
Crayon rubbings 1005.C
Creative cllctn 1009.F
Critical thinking 1011.F

D
Decision chart 1011.B
Decision making 1011.B
Decision West 1008.K
Decoding 1004.F
Deliberate work 1002.H
Democracy 1008.A
Design, room 1010.E
Desk list 1003.D

Detectives fix 1002.A
Diagram flower 1011.G
Diagram pndlm 1007.H
Diagram, science 1011.G
Digital time 1006.G
Dinosaur report 1005.IH
Diploma, none 1012.A
Disagreements 1008.D
Discipline 1010.G
Discipline Native 1008.C
Discover 10 Fact 1006.A
Distinct answers 1001.C
Diversity, answers 1001.C
Domino effect 1001.C
Dot game 1003.G
Dr. Ben Carson 1004.G
Dr. Seuss 1004.E

E
Earthquake 1007.H
Eddie spelling 1003.D
Edison, Thomas 1007.E
Editors, student 1002.D
Electric bulb 1007.E
Ellie math 1002.H
Environment CH 10
Estimation leaves 1007.E
Evaluation ques. 1011.D
Executive branch 1008.A
Expert Exchange 1008.F

F
Fairness 1010.I

Famous people 1008.J
Feedback loop 1007.G
Field trip zoo 1008.A
Figuring formulas 1006.E
Finger multiplication 1006.D
First gr. Authors 1005.E
First time writer 1005.F
Fiscus tree 1010.G
Fish aquarium 1007.D
Fish bat snake 1007.D
Five day stories 1005.G
Flash cards, facts 1006.C
Floor letters 1005.A
Florrie, dear 1012.H
Folded paper 1011.G
Food coloring 1007.G
Force fit 1009.F
Formulas, math 1006.E
Four basic steps 1001.B
Four boys 1002.F
Frac. color list 1006.H
Fraction compar. 1006.I
Fraction cutouts 1006.H
Fragrances 1010.D
Frog sentences 1005.C

G

Games, indoor 1003.G
Gardner, Dr. 1011.I
GED 1011.A
Geniuses 1011.I
Geometry 1006.E
George 1003.B
Glitches reading 1004.H

Good spellers 1003.D
Grace 1003.B
Grade fast! 1005.K
Grade level 1003.B
Grammar fixes 1002.A
Graphics 2-D 1011.G
Gratitude 1010.H
Gratitude career 1012.H
Grid 'X' facts 1006.C

H

Haiku, seasons 1005.J
Hall walking 1009.B
Hancock, John 1008.J
Harry Potter 1004.F
Height of tree 1006.J
Held back 1002.F
Henderson laughter 1003.A
Henrich rsrch 1002.B
High IQ 1003.A
High school tchr 1002.C
Hirsch, J.D. 1012.A
Honesty 1010.J
Horse 1011.F
How child learns 1011.H
How read begins 1004.F
Howard deliberate 1002.H
Humor and intellig. 1003.A

I

Identify teams 1009.E
Implications how 1004.B.
Implications use 1011.F

Individualize	1003.C	Lesson washout	1012.G
Indoor games	1003.G	Letters, red yarn	1005.A
IQ and laughter	1003.A	Levels AVK	1011.H
IQs can go up	1003.A	Levels Bloom 123	1011.C
Intelligence, art	1010.A	Levels Bloom 456	1011.D
Intelligence, scent	1010.D	Lining up	1010.I
Intelligences 7	1011.I	Long addition	1006.B
ITBS	1010.F	Lost money	1010.J
Intra-per. intell.	1011.I	Loving discipline	1010.H
Inter-per. intell.	1011.I		

J

Jack, Beanstalk	1004.C		
Jimmy	1009.E		
Justin as 'Alexa'	1012.D		

M

		Majority rule	1008.C
		M&Ms	1009.B

K

Keys to teach.	1001.B	Mandan Indians	1008.E
Kindness, ABCD	1009.C	Maori children	1005.B
Kinesthetic learners	1011.H	Map 3 pigs	1011.G
Knowledge ques.	1011.C	Maple syrup trip	1010.K
Kristie's think.	1003.B	Market place	1008.H
		Math 'fixes'	1002.A

L

		Math intelligence	1011.I
Laughter .. IQ	1003.A	Math patterns	1006.C
Leaf rubbings	1007.B	Mary - piano	1011.I
Learning AKV	1011.H	Measure bubbles	1007.F
Learning styles	1011.H	Memorization	1004.D
Leaves alike?	1007.A	Miller, old	1004.B
Leaves ..trees	1007.B	Mind map	1011.G
Lectures	1001.D	Mistakes, fix	1002.A
Lesson design	1001.A	Monotone test	1003.E
Lesson overview	1001.B	Mood, teacher's	1010.L
		Morris School	1010.E
		Moths	1007.C
		Multiplication	1006.C
		Music, classical	1010.B

Music sub's plan — 1001.A
Mysteries, solve — 1003.I

N

Nails.. horse — 1011.F
Native American — 1008.C
Never wrote — 1005.F
New Zealand — 1005.B
Niagara painting — 1010.A
9-1-1 — 1010.J
Nine pattern — 1006.C
Nineteen no diploma — 1012.A
1910 multi. — 1006.D
Number wizard — 1011.I
Numbers, assign — 1009.A

O

Observation ants — 1007.I
Old Miller — 1004.B
One minute — 1009.A
Onc room sclhouse — 1008.I
Open-end ques. — 1001.C
Optometrist — 1003.A
Oregon Trail — 1008.K
Organization — 1011.F
Original rsrch — 1007.I
Osmosis — 1007.G
Outline 3 pigs — 1011.G

P

Pat on own back — 1005.A
Pencil circles — 1003.D
Pendulums — 1007.H

People genius — 1011.I
Petition, board — 1008.B
Phases, reading — 1004.G
Phillips, Mr. — 1002.G
Philosopher genius — 1011.I
Photos to poetry — 1005.I
Piaget — 1005.A
Piano, Mary — 1011.I
Pigs, 3 Little 123 — 1011.C
Pigs, 3 Little 456 — 1011.D
Plan everything — 1011.A
Plant time line — 1011.G
Plastic chips — 1006.A
Play 2nd Grade — 1002.E
Poem, answer — 1001.G
Poem booklet — 1005.J
Poetry photos — 1005.I
Poisons — 1002.E
Polar Bear — 1007.J
Police visit — 1010.J
Praise — 1010.H
Precise work — 1002.H
Predicting — 1007.E
Presentations — 1001.D
Primary rsrch — 1007.I
Principal's impact — 1010.F
Private papers — 1009.A
Problem solving — 1011.D

Q

Q&A study tip — 1011.C
One room — 1008.I
Question and ans. — 1011.C

Questions, game	1003.G	Schoolhouse	1008.I
Quotations	1010.C	Science plans	1007.F
		Science play	1002.F
R		Science teachers	1002.C
Race car story	1004.F	Seasons, haiku	1005.J
Read by dictating	1004.A	Second gr. play	1002.E
Reading circle	1004.C	Secretary of State	1007.D
Reading glitches	1004.H	Seize the day	1002.G
Reading implica.	1004.B	Sentences, 2 to 22	1005.C
Reading phases	1004.G	Seuss Revisited	1004.E
Reading stages	1004.F	Seventh gr math	1001.E
Recall	1004.G	Sharpeners	1006.G
Reddington rsch	1002.B	Shannon's reading	1003.B
Reduce problems	1011.A	Shawn and camp	1010.H
Report, dinosaur	1005.H	Shout Out!	1003.D
Research def.	1007.I	Shy child	1003.F
Research, orig.	1007.I	Sick child 1010.K	1012.E
Research, sec.	1008.E	Sight words	1004.G
Reverse engineering	1007.G	Signals, silent	1010.G
Revolution song	1009.B	Silent clapping	1010.G
Rewards	1008.D	Silverstein	1004.D
Rich, Mr.	1010.H	Skipping a grade	1002.F
Richard compasn	1012.C	Slide show	1005.I
Rick diploma	1012.A	Smart w/Bloom 123	1011.C
River, Diego	1010.F	Smart w/Bloom 456	1011.D
Rob ... old miller	1004.B	Snake, bat, fish	1007.D
Roman Empire	1008.G	Socratic teaching	1012.G
Room design	1010.E	Song	1010.B
Rubric grading	1005.L	Spelling sentences	1003.D
S		Spelling tactics	1003.D
Sailboating	1001.D	Spiders	1010.D
Save the sub	1001.A	Split times facts	1006.C
School board	1008.B	Shel Silverstein	1004.D
		Sound whiz genius	1011.I

Stages in reading 1004.F
Steitzer, principal 1010.F
Steps to teaching 1001.B
Student detectives 1002.A
Student editors 1002.D
Students science 1002.C
Students tch math 1001.E
Student teaching 1012.G
Students as teachers 1002.C
Students' .. mood 1010.L
Students write ?? 123 1011.C
Students write ?? 456 1011.D
Study questions 1011.F
Study teams 1009.E
Study tip Q&A 1011.G
Styles of lrning 1011.H
Substitute's lesson 1001.A
Success four boys 1002.F
Success pathways 1002.H
Summarize 1001.F
Summer for Tom 1012.B
Surpass sameness 1003.C
Suzy's money 1010.J
Syllable glitch 1004.H
Synthesis ques. 1011.D

T
Taffy 1003.E
Tapping foot 1011.H
Teacher's mood 1010.L
Teaching steps 1001.B
Teams of two 1009.E
Ten facts addi. 1006.A

Terrariums 1007.D
Test cover up 1010.E
Test 'fix its' 1002.A
Test monotone 1003.E
Test questions 1011.E
Theme lists 1003.D
Think tank 1011.F
Thinkers…games 1003.G
Thinking levels 1,2,3 1011.C
Thinking levels 4,5,6 1011.D
Third gr. writers 1005.F
Three pigs Bloom 1011.C
Three pigs outline 1011.E
Ticking clock 1011.H
Tiffany's eyes 1004.H
Time Line 1011.G
Time, Telling 1006.G
Tom formulas 1006.E
Tommy changes 1012.B
Treasure box NZ 1005.B
Tree height 1006.J
Tree leaves alike 1007.A
Tribal discipline 1008.C
Trust factor 1010.K
Tutoring spelling 1003.D
20 Questions 1003.H
2 to 22 Words 1005.C

V
Validate reading 1004.C
Variety answers 1001.C
Verbal intelligence 1011.I
Video lesson 1001.A
Visitors, bug 1007.C

Visual intelligence	1011.I
Visual learning	1011.H
Visualize	1004.F
Vocabulary work	1003.D

W

War signals	1010.G
Warner, Sylvia	1005.B
Wars, disagree.	1008.D
Washout lesson	1012.G
Webbing	1012.G
Whirl wind genius	1011.I
Whisper method	1010.J
Williams, Mr.	1001.E
Willingness, fair	1010.I
Words NZ	1005.B
Words, syllables	1003.A
Wordsmith genius	1011.I
WWII	1008.D
Write to read	1004.A
Writing check off	1005.L
Writing, copy	1005.D
Written by 2nd	1002.E
Writers, 3rd grade	1005.F

Y

Yarn letters	1005.A
Yellow car	1004.B
Yorktown exchange	1008.F

Z

| Zoo field trip | 1008.C |

MEET THE AUTHOR

Trudi Carter earned her Bachelor of Science degree at Oswego, New York and her Master of Arts degree in Iowa. Carter taught grades 1st to 8th from New York to Iowa to Georgia. Keeping abreast of university education innovations, individualized research-based materials are developed to create independent learners.

Experimenting with high levels of student participation embedded with complex thinking skills, students learn research skills, identify related questions, and teach their findings to their classmates.

Working with academically and creatively gifted students in a pull out program, students become thoroughly independent learners by taking charge of their work assignments.

A personalized tutoring business based on thinking analysis proves that children improve more quickly when assignments are clearly defined and focused on the child's grade level.

A 3 week immersion course for the 'extreme gifted' at the University of Iowa with Dr. Nicolas Colangelo leads to becoming a Talents Unlimited trainer. Based on an intense business training course by international trainer Libyan Cassone, Carter developed a unique teacher/training course for business trainers used at an energy plant and a 'creative training' company.

Today, Carter prepares materials *to pass it forward* to the next generation. Her vision is a renaissance in authentic learning based on an appreciation and application of one's personal talents to benefit everyone worldwide.

A Student's Perspective

I feel very privileged to have had Trudi Carter as my tutor growing up. Perhaps more than any other teacher I've had, she saw my potential and devoted her time and attention to helping me bring it forth. She had a wonderful ability to recognize my unique learning style and engaged me through my interest in a way that made learning both effective and fun. Trudi is Master Educator, a Teacher of Teachers, and I am grateful for our continued friendship.

Dillon Siewert

One looks back with appreciation
to the brilliant teachers, but with gratitude to those
who touched our human feelings.
The curriculum is so much necessary raw material,
but warmth is the vital element
for the growing plant and the soul of the child.
Carl Jung

Sources

Online Quotes from www.brainyquotes.com

PublicDomainImages.net

Copyright Requirements Observed

The Metropolitan Museum of Art,
New York City
Open Access means art is considered
free and in the public domain.

Edited by

Nina Riccio

and

Bruce F. Carter

ISBN
978-1-66640-543-9

www.ingramcontent.com/pod-product-compliance
Lightning Source LLC
Chambersburg PA
CBHW060007100426
42740CB00010B/1430